Qualitative Interviewing

BLOOMSBURY RESEARCH METHODS

Edited by Mark Elliot and Jessica Nina Lester

The Bloomsbury Research Methods series provides authoritative introductions to key and emergent research methods across a range of disciplines.

Each book introduces the key elements of a particular method and/or methodology and includes examples of its application. Written in an accessible style by leading experts in the field, this series is an innovative pedagogical and research resource.

Also available in the series

Forthcoming in the series

RESEARCH METHODS

Qualitative Interviewing

ROSALIND EDWARDS AND JANET HOLLAND

BLOOMSBURY ACADEMIC
LONDON • NEW YORK • OXFORD • NEW DELHI • SYDNEY

BLOOMSBURY ACADEMIC
Bloomsbury Publishing Plc
50 Bedford Square, London, WC1B 3DP, UK
1385 Broadway, New York, NY 10018, USA
29 Earlsfort Terrace, Dublin 2, Ireland

BLOOMSBURY, BLOOMSBURY ACADEMIC and the Diana logo are trademarks
of Bloomsbury Publishing Plc

First published in Great Britain 2013
This edition published 2023

Series design by Charlotte James
Cover image © shuoshu / iStock

A catalogue record for this book is available from the British Library.

A catalog record for this book is available from the Library of Congress.

ISBN: HB: 978-1-3502-7513-3
PB: 978-1-3502-7512-6
ePDF: 978-1-3502-7515-7
eBook: 978-1-3502-7514-0

Series: Bloomsbury Research Methods

Typeset by Deanta Global Publishing Services, Chennai, India
Printed and bound in Great Britain

To find out more about our authors and books visit www.bloomsbury.com and
sign up for our newsletters.

CONTENTS

FIGURES

SERIES EDITORS' FOREWORD

The idea behind this series is a simple one: to provide concise and accessible overviews of a range of frequently used research methods and of current issues in research methodology. Books in the series have been written by experts in their fields with a brief to write about their subject for a broad audience who are assumed to be interested but not necessarily to have any prior knowledge. The series is a natural outgrowth of the 'What is?' strand at Economic and Social Research Council Research Methods Festivals, which have proved popular both at the festivals themselves and subsequently as a resource on the website of the ESRC National Centre for Research Methods.

Methodological innovation is the order of the day, and the 'What is?' format allows researchers who are new to a field to gain an insight into its key features, while also providing a useful update on recent developments for people who have had some prior acquaintance with it. All readers should find it helpful to be taken through the discussion of key terms, the history of how the method or methodological issue has developed and the assessment of the strengths and possible weaknesses of the approach through the analysis of illustrative examples.

In the new edition of *Qualitative Interviewing*, Rosalind Edwards and Janet Holland provide an updated discussion of what remains one of the most popular qualitative research methods in the social sciences, that is, the qualitative interview. The authors point to the long-standing popularity, history and challenges of this method, while noting the ways in which the method has grown and changed in response to new understandings, technological developments and historical events (e.g. Covid-19 pandemic). Like the first edition of the book, the authors describe the kinds of phenomena an interview allows for a social science researcher to explore. They also point to how new technologies have opened up new spaces for where and how interviews might be conducted. Indeed, there are now many different places that one might conduct an interview. From walking interviews to various online methods, Edwards and Holland point to how, where and how one conducts an interview inevitably shapes the nature of the data and the interaction between the participant and interviewer. While interviewing methods have historically centred on asking questions, the authors point to new, contemporary tools for eliciting understanding, such as to various textual, visual and creative methods. While Edwards and Holland outline a compelling set of reasons and ways to conduct qualitative interviews, they also offer important theoretical, ethical and practical critiques and challenges. They describe, for instance, how Indigenous perspectives challenge in important and critical ways the standard conceptions of qualitative interviews, as well as overview how power and emotion are always at play in an interview context. Considered as a whole, what this book offers is a cutting-edge overview of qualitative interviewing practices; one that is positioned in a contemporary research context and brings to the fore how emerging ethical, technological, and methodological considerations might inform how social science researchers plan for and conduct qualitative interviews.

Jessica Nina Lester & Mark Elliot
Series editors

ACKNOWLEDGEMENTS

The second edition of this book builds on our many years of experience of doing qualitative interviews but also more recently on our engagements with new challenges and developments since the first edition. These include interview-based research during the Covid-19 pandemic and discussions with Indigenous social researchers. Thank you to all the people who we have interviewed and also to all our qualitative research colleagues, from whom we have learnt a great deal.

CHAPTER 1

Qualitative Interviews – The Key Terms

Introduction

Interviews are ubiquitous in everyday life. We have all been interviewed, at school, at university, for jobs, in a medical setting, and have seen or read interviews with others. We know the format, what to do and how to do it. Modern or postmodern society has been called the 'interview', or even the 'confessional' society, the latter calling up a particular type of interview where intimate matters may be revealed (Atkinson and Silverman 1997). Most of us are probably familiar with the role of interviewee, but many of us also will have undertaken interviews ourselves, and most of these will have been qualitative interviews in the broadest sense, one person asking another person questions on a particular topic or issue and the other responding. We will also know from our own experience that these interviews can differ widely, from the confidential probing of the medical interview in a (relatively) private space, through the publicity-oriented celebrity interview, to the perhaps aggressive questioning of a politician by a news journalist. So clearly both the immediate and the broader social context are relevant to the way the interview will be conducted, experienced and understood.

In this book, we want to move from our everyday experience and understanding of the characteristics of the interview to the use of the qualitative interview as a methodological and research tool in social science. The interview is probably the most widely used method employed in qualitative research. Qualitative interviews have been the basis for many important studies across a range of disciplinary fields, but understandings of what it means to carry out such interviews have shifted over time in line with ebbs and flows in the prominence of particular philosophical approaches to understanding the social world and how it works (discussed in Chapter 2). These ebbs and flows have led to changing conceptions of the researcher, as objective and so able to access objective knowledge about the interviewee and their social world; as implicated in the processes at play in the interview in a range of ways that affect their understanding of the knowledge that can be produced in the interview; or as an advocate speaking for or giving voice to the interviewee. One key set of scholarly exchanges has been over the 'radical critique' of interviews. The radical critique argues that interviews are not a method of grasping the unmediated experiences of research participants – that is, the content of the interview data. Rather, the enactment of the method, of interviewer and interviewee exchanges, is data – that is, the form. Some see the focus on form as posing an unbridgeable divide between the experienced and the expressed, and call for attention to the ways that interview data may be used to discuss the social world beyond the interview encounter (content) (Hughes et al. 2020), while others urge reflexive analytic attention to interviews as speech events because there cannot be content without form (Whitaker and Atkinson 2020). Debates around such issues are explored in this book.

A major theme coursing through the book relates to how to approach research and particular methodological tools, such as the qualitative interview which is the focus of this book. In general, the use of a particular method should be derived from the research topic, the research questions to which an answer is sought and the theoretical framework within which the researcher is working. The researcher moves from research concern and topic to research questions, to appropriate method or methods via their underpinning philosophical stance and theoretical approach to understanding the social world, so constructing their methodology (Blaikie and Priest 2019; Mason 2018).

The chapters of the book will describe the different forms that qualitative interviews can take and the kinds of tools or aids to discussion that can be used during interviews, always linking back to the topic and aims of the research being carried out, and its underpinning philosophical approach. The practicalities of qualitative interviewing are as ever undergoing change with the availability of new technologies but are also subject to enduring issues around asking questions and listening to the answers and the implications of the underlying power dynamics of broader social relations for research and interviewer–interviewee relations. Transcription – the rendition of the aural material generated from interviews into text – is noted in Chapters 2 and 8. The application of methods of analysis in order to make meaning from the aural-textual material is covered in other texts (e.g. Gibbs 2018).

In this chapter, we provide definitions of qualitative interviews and discuss debates about changing descriptions of the interviewee as 'research subjects', 'interviewee', 'respondent' or 'participant'. We briefly discuss samples and cases in qualitative interviews and review the changing wider social/economic context in which qualitative interviews are conducted. The chapter sets the scene for the book to follow.

What Is a Qualitative Interview?

Most textbooks will tell you that interviews range through a continuum, from structured, through semi-structured, to unstructured (or focused) interviews (Blaikie and Priest 2019; Bryman 2019). The structured interview is at the quantitative end of the scale and is more used in survey approaches. The rest of the scale, semi-structured and unstructured, is the area occupied by qualitative researchers, with the interviews characterized by increasing levels of flexibility and lack of structure. Many of the terms you will have discovered applied to qualitative interviewing appear in this part of the continuum, for example, in-depth, informal, non-directed, open-ended, conversational, naturalistic, narrative, biographical, oral or life history, ethnographic and many more discussed in Chapter 3. The terms used for any particular interview type relate to the underlying philosophy and specific approach taken to research, discussed further in Chapter 2.

Jennifer Mason argues that, despite the large variations in style and tradition, all qualitative interviewing has certain core features in common:

1. The interactional exchange of dialogue (between two or more participants, in person or through a range of other modes of communication).

2. A thematic, topic-centred, biographical or narrative approach where the researcher has topics, themes or issues they wish to cover but with a fluid and flexible structure.

3. A perspective regarding knowledge as situated and contextual, requiring the researcher to ensure that relevant contexts are brought into focus so that the situated knowledge can be produced. Meanings and understandings are created in an interaction, which is effectively a co-production, involving the construction or reconstruction of knowledge. (Adapted from Mason 2018: 110.)

Kathryn Roulston (2019) refers to research interviews as a 'social practice', as interactions that are accomplished by those involved. These interactions can call up wider social dynamics of power and identity management, invoke role-playing and turn-taking, involve moments of miscommunication and others of rapport and include laughter and tears (see Chapters 5 and 7 especially). The interview, then, is a complex interactional achievement.

The 'Subject' of Research

What those who are being researched are called are not just neutral terms but also indicate ways of thinking about them and how they are understood as relating to the interview and consequently reflect the philosophical stance of the researcher. Terms for the researched have included subject, respondent, informant, interviewee and participant, the sequence here suggesting a movement from passive to active. The subject is typical of the close-ended, structured interview, matched by an interviewer who is expected to introduce no biases into the research and data and deliver objectivity by asking the same questions in the same way to all those who appear for the interview, ignoring as far as possible the subjectivity of the subject. Criticisms of this position come from those who are interested in the views, understandings and subjectivities of the people they research in differing ways, including those who take interpretive, transformative, postmodern and realist approaches, all discussed in Chapter 2.

Historically, respondents and informants have been associated with ethnographic methods, where key figures are sought when researching particular groups or cultures, to provide useful information on the community being studied. Participant emerges from this field approach too and applies specifically to the researcher in a method typical of ethnography: participant observation. Here, the researcher is still an outsider, although hoping to become more of an insider or more accepted, by participating in the activities of the group being researched. Interviewee is matched by interviewer, the similarity of terms suggesting more equality in the research relationship. Participant takes this further and carries with it from interpretivist and transformative positions certain understandings of the part played by the researched and the researcher. Participation in research can empower the interviewee; for example, many feminists have sought to give voice in their research to those, particularly women, who have been unheard or silenced in earlier social science research (Hesse-Biber 2021). From this perspective, reflexivity is called for in the researcher, who must recognize themselves as part of both the research process and the power relations that permeate the research encounter of the qualitative interview. Both researcher and researched bring with them concepts, ideas, theories, values, experiences and multiply intersecting identities, all of which can play a part in research interaction in the qualitative interview.

The terms used for participants in research reflect the different underlying philosophical positions adopted. Broadly they cover ideas about the neutral interviewer, standardization and exclusion of bias at the heart of more positivist approaches, to ideas of reflexive construction, difference and shifting positionalities of the researcher and the researched that have emerged from feminist, postmodern and interpretivist stances, as outlined in Chapter 2. Throughout this book, we use terms such as researcher and interviewer and interviewee, participant, respondent and subject, according to the context in which they occur.

Sampling and Cases in Qualitative Interviewing

Strategies for selecting who to interview in qualitative research have suffered a similar problem to qualitative research in general with the representative random probability samples of quantitative research regarded as the norm against which qualitative research should be measured and so found wanting. It is odd to talk of a sampling or cases in qualitative social research without a context since whom you research and interview is dependent on the nature and design of your study. Some would argue that even the term sample is inappropriate, given that the focus of data generation in qualitative research is on the process rather than an end point of numbers. Others, such as Nick Emmel (2013), regard the term 'sampling' as inappropriate because it invokes social phenomena as somehow independent of the researcher's account of them; to be picked (sampled) from a pre-existing social context. Rather, taking a realist perspective (see Chapter 2), the researcher identifies and chooses cases that will help them to build (provisional) causal explanations of how mechanisms work in particular social context, relations and circumstances.

Whether you are sampling or choosing cases, your strategy must provide the data you need to produce answers to your research questions, and the sort of questions you pose will be shaped by your understanding of the relationship between theory and data. In grounded theory approaches, explanation is generated from the empirical context. The term 'theoretical sampling' was introduced by Glaser and Strauss (1967) in the context of the development of grounded theory, and over time definitions and practices of both theoretical sampling and grounded theory have been modified by Strauss and others (Corbin and Strauss 2014). Many qualitative researchers use this approach to sampling without necessarily accepting the techniques and strategies advocated by Strauss and colleagues, nor indeed the specific relationship with grounded theory. Another, more general, way of thinking about theoretical sampling in qualitative research is that selection is made on the basis of relevance to producing a sample that will enable you to develop and test your emerging theoretical ideas. This form of sampling may shade into a more purposeful form of sampling. Purposive sampling is pragmatic, driven by the empirical focus so as to allow the researcher to answer their research questions. Research participants are selected strategically because they have the life experience to provide rich information and throw particular light on the issue under investigation (Patton 2017). Often qualitative researchers are working with a reflexive interplay between theoretical and empirical concerns in identifying their samples or cases.

One pragmatic strategy through which sampling can be developed is snowballing, a process in which contact is made with participants appropriate for your research through whatever access route you can find, and through these first participants you are introduced to others of similar/relevant characteristics for your research. This can often be an integral part of ethnography, which involves spending time in the field with the group under study, but is also useful in contacting hard-to-reach groups and individuals (Parker et al. 2019). This approach may be part of a convenience sample strategy – available by means of accessibility. Indeed, many social science investigations take place on university students, educational practitioners undertake educational research in their own schools and classrooms, and people pursue ethnography on a group of which they are already a part, because it is convenient.

The issue of 'how many' should be in a qualitative sample is a common question among students hoping to undertake research and will be discussed in Chapter 6. For now, it is interesting to note the issues around samples and cases raised in qualitative longitudinal research, which takes place through time, typically involving repeat interviews at intervals with the same individuals or groups. In relation to sample size, for example, the sample might fall in size due to death or people dropping out or it might grow if, for example, you are following a family and a child becomes old enough to be interviewed as well as their parent/s. Clearly, the number of interviews is not the same as the number of cases in this instance. Your procedure for generating a sample will similarly be based on the design, aims and philosophy of your research. And for each member of the sample, you will have multiple interviews and considerably more data than you would have from a one-off, snapshot study that might require methods of analysis that can address extensive amounts of qualitative data: 'big qual' (Davidson et al. 2019).

The Broad Social Context of Qualitative Interviews

The broad social context of qualitative research, and so interviews, is multifaceted. The regulations and standards laid down for the conduct of research constitute the research governance regime (further discussed in Chapter 2). Thus, the institution in which the researcher is located will require good practice in research, and an appropriate approach to risk and ethical considerations, particularly in relation to institutional liability. In the personal interaction of the qualitative interview, ethical guidelines (institutional and professional) require no harm to come to participants. The emphasis on ethical practice in the social sciences has been on the researched, with ethical considerations based on protecting them from risk and exploitation and gaining informed consent for the research (see Chapter 6). But there has also been some attention to the impact of qualitative interviewing on the researcher's risk and safety, and emotional labour and well-being, with gender and race as features (e.g. Bashir 2020; McClelland 2017; Moran and Asquith 2020). We discuss emotional issues in interviewing, as well as power in interviews, in Chapter 7.

For the qualitative researcher seeking to undertake interviews for a particular piece of research, an important immediate context relates to the social relations of the specific field into which the researcher is about to plunge, with its multiple and often contradictory demands. The interviewer might need to navigate and negotiate in a school, a factory, a large or small organization, a university and a prison (see the discussion in Chapter 4 about where qualitative interviews may be conducted). Access and negotiation might take place with a small social group or network, a group of members of a political movement or among members of a particular sporting 'tribe'; the list is endless as is the complexity of the social interactions involved.

Conclusion

We have suggested that interviews are ubiquitous in society today, and this is a broad context within which qualitative research using particular types of interviews will be taking place. This can be a help and a hindrance. Prospective participants will have ideas about what is expected and required in an interview, which might be helpful but might also shape their behaviour in ways that can be a hindrance. It is important for qualitative researchers to be able to draw their participants onto the terrain of the research interview, for them to understand what the research is about, and how the interview will differ from others of which they might have experienced. We discuss these sorts of practicalities in conducting interviews in Chapter 6.

We have introduced you to qualitative interviews and the terms used to describe them, given an indication of the various understandings of the relationship between the researcher and the researched and its connection with the philosophical positions that underpin research and indicated where these issues are recurrent themes or will be discussed further in individual chapters in the book. In Chapter 2, we move on to the emergence and history of qualitative interviewing.

CHAPTER 2

The Development of Qualitative Interviews

Introduction

The systematic use of interviews as a social research method in their own right (rather than part of observation, for example), to explore people's understandings of their lives and aspects of their experiences, is relatively recent, from the mid-twentieth century. Throughout that time, there has been a constant interplay between epistemological or philosophical ideas about the nature of social life and our ability to know about it and how interviews are thought about and practised. Key issues that have woven themselves throughout the history of qualitative interviews are debates about what should be or is the relationship between researchers, the researched and the research. These have manifest themselves in debates about foundations and truth; bias and standardization; reflexivity and construction; and difference and power, among others. Interviews are not, in themselves, inherently biased or unbiased, oppressive or progressive and so on; rather it is the philosophical approach underpinning them that in large part creates such debates.

As well as shifting philosophical stances shaping understandings of the practice of qualitative interviews, research governance procedures and technologies have also played their part in possibilities for and debates about the relationship between researchers, the researched and the research.

Histories of Qualitative Interviews

Qualitative research, as an acknowledged and systematic approach to knowledge creation, has its roots in the anthropology and sociology of the early decades of the twentieth century (e.g. Malinowski 1922; Mead 1935; Park and Burgess 1925). Norman Denzin and Yvonne Lincoln (2017) argue that qualitative social research as a field of enquiry in its own right in North America has operated within eight or nine historical 'moments' across the twentieth century and into the twenty-first. A traditional moment associated with a positivist, foundational paradigm stressing objectivity and verification held sway between 1900 and 1950. The modernist or golden age moment of maintaining procedural formalism that was dominant from 1950 to 1970, and the blurred genres moment that saw the rise to the prevalence of post-positivist interpretive perspectives during 1970 and 1980, led to a period of paradigm wars during 1980–5. The blurring of genres, where qualitative research drew on humanities methodologies, prompted a crisis of representation that peaked between 1986 and 1990, as researchers grappled with how they might acknowledge values and social divisions and write themselves and their subjects into their texts. The postmodern moment of 1990–5 and experimental inquiry moment of 1995–2000 saw the continued movement away from foundational and quasi-foundational approaches to qualitative research, as researchers sought alternative, evocative, moral, critical and located methods of research and writing, and evaluative criteria by which to legitimate their work. This brings us into the methodologically contested present of 2000–2004 and paradigm proliferation of 2005–10, seeing pulls between evidence-based ideas and active political engagement. A now and future moment, from 2010 on, is – say Denzin and Lincoln – seeing the critical and reflexive form of messiness, uncertainty, multivocality and intertextuality become more common in qualitative research.

Denzin and Lincoln acknowledge that these historical moments are somewhat artificial and stress that they are a complex historical field, crosscutting and overlapping, reconfiguring and hybridizing, over time. As we delve into later in this chapter, within the various broader shifting philosophical approaches to which Denzin and Lincoln refer, qualitative interviewing aims to achieve and means different things.

Denzin and Lincoln assert that they are not presenting a progress narrative since all the waves are circulating and competing in the present eighth/ninth moment, but it is difficult not to read their work as a celebration of the emergence of multiple modes of knowing and transformative research approaches. The moments themselves seem to follow Anthony Giddens' image of a 'runaway world' in late or high modernity (2011) as they speed up during the latter part of the twentieth century and into the first decade of the twenty-first. Perhaps dramatic and constant change appears to us to be the motif of the time period that we are living through, while the past seems to be more stable. Marja Alastalo, for example, points to the 'quite remarkable changes' (2008: 30) that occurred in qualitative methods during the 1920s. The case study method, as qualitative research was usually referred to at the time, came to be regarded as an approach in its own right, often in opposition to the statistical method (though some also saw them as complementary). The idea of 'the case study method' then faded, with the concept of qualitative research and methods emerging post the Second World War.

Looking specifically at qualitative interviews and broadly echoing Denzin and Lincoln's depiction of the direction of historical movements entailed in the crisis of representation, Svend Brinkmann and Steiner Kvale (2015) refer to a shift in understanding the interview using metaphors of miner or traveller for the interviewer. The data miner, or modernist interviewer, is seeking to uncover nuggets of truth through interviews; a seam of knowledge that is 'out there', ready to be gathered up. The data traveller, or postmodern interviewer, embarks upon an interactive and reflective interpretation of how they came to 'see' and transform particular 'sights' into knowledge. Also in line with Denzin, Brinkmann and Kvale clearly prefer the postmodern traveller but acknowledge the presence of the modernist miner operating in the qualitative research interview landscape at the same time. Indeed, the different positions in the contemporary radical critique of interviews debate referred to in Chapter 1 invoke the distinction between the miner collecting knowledge and the traveller generating knowledge.

An alternative view of shifts in the understanding and practice of qualitative interviews is offered by Mike Savage (2010). In the context of a steady growth in qualitative research since the late 1950s/ early 1960s in Britain, Savage identifies 'a distinctive break between what I term "gentlemanly" social science (as a means of making its masculine and bourgeois aspects explicit) which prevailed in 1950, and an emergent professional and "demoralized" social science which was ascending by the mid-1960s' (12). He makes the case that the 1960s was a period in which the specifically sociological qualitative interview about everyday life was emergent practice in uncharted territory. While researchers had a clear sense of their own importance, there was a lack of clarity in researcher–researched relationships and how they were to treat each other. British social researchers of the early 1960s had not yet come to distinguish their visual observation from the research subjects' elicited narratives in interviews. Observational comments on the interviewees – their appearance, attitudes and behaviour – were regarded as much a means of accessing knowledge as the interviewees' words – a process that placed the interviewer as an intellectual and moral authority. In contrast, Savage asserts, contemporary research practice removes the subject as physicality (or at least the researcher's view of it) and turns them into professional text. Ironically then, the avoidance of making explicit value judgements about research subjects has resulted in the researcher hiding their own evaluative imprint.

Conceptions about the place of the researcher in relation to the social world generally and the people who they interview specifically vary according to the philosophical approach that they take in conducting their research.

Interviews through Different Philosophical Lenses

In what follows, we attempt briefly to introduce a range of philosophical approaches to knowledge that underpin its production, to show how they conceptualize interviews in different ways and to consider the implications of this. Our intention is not to offer comprehensive coverage of all possible philosophies that inform social research but rather to demonstrate that interviews signify different possibilities in relation to the generation of knowledge dependent on the approach.

Positivism and Interviews

Positivism is not a simple or single concept, and there is no completely shared understanding of the idea. Nevertheless, the main features of positivism are that it distinguishes between the external world and the observer experiencing it, uses observable evidence and employs objectivity in separating out value-free knowledge gained through systematic procedures from beliefs, feelings and moral stance (Williams 2016). Positivism's stress on objective reality and truth, as distinct from subjective and varied understandings, means that the production of knowledge is regarded as replicable and thus able to be tried and tested. Some forms of grounded theory (see Chapter 1), and evidence-based and evaluative research, are examples of approaches that take the external world as independently knowable and are warranted through a form of positivism.

What is called a foundational approach is taken to the purpose and process of interviews, where knowledge is deductive, objective and value free. Access to truth and thus to knowledge is through adhering to tried and tested rules of method that are universally applicable, regardless of context. Such an approach may involve standardization, where the researcher ensures that all interviewees are asked the same questions in the same ways. More crucial, however, is the elimination or at the very least minimization of any influence from the researcher, based on concerns that qualitative interviews can lack objectivity and be subject to bias. For accurate data to be obtained in an interview and in the analysis, researchers need to be impartial and not contaminate an interviewee's report of their activities and experiences. Overall, a positivist approach to interviews demands a conception of questions as stimulus and answers as response.

The use of interviews is referred to as 'collecting' data in a positivist approach because the material is regarded as a report on a reality that is independent of the interviewee. Brinkmann and Kvale's metaphor of the interviewer as miner captures this approach to interviewing. Further, because it reflects an independent reality, the data gathered in interviews will be verifiable – interviewees' accounts of behaviour or events either being truthful and reliable or misleading and distorted. An interviewee's account can be checked for credibility, for example, by comparing what he or she says with the researcher's own observations, or official records, or the accounts of other people who were involved in the situation or event (often referred to as triangulation).

A direct contrast to this assertion of a distinction between observable fact and subjective meaning, and a mechanistic conception of the interview process, can be found in interpretive approaches to how the social world works and how people can know about it.

Interpretive Approaches and Interviews

Interpretivism covers a broad range of different phenomenological philosophical approaches (constructivism, symbolic interactionism, ethnomethodology, etc.) that are all loosely concerned with understanding social phenomena from the perspectives of those involved. Thus in this approach, knowledge takes the form of explanations of how others interpret and make sense of their day-to-day life and interactions (Yanow and Schwartz-Shea 2014).

As human interaction and negotiation is seen as the basis for the creation and understanding of social life in interpretive approaches, it is the interaction of the participants in the interview situation – the researcher and the researched – that generates knowledge. The data in the form of talk that comprises the interview is regarded as a co-construction – what Brinkmann and Kvale call a literal *inter-view*. Brinkmann and Kvale's metaphor of the interviewer as traveller gains purchase in these approaches. It does not reach complete fulfilment in many interpretive approaches, however, because there is still a sense that interviewees can recount and convey to the researcher experiences and feelings that are part of their social world beyond the interview – an issue at stake in the radical critique of interviews debate that we discussed in Chapter 1.

Methodological discussions by interpretive researchers can draw attention to the interview as a co-production of meaning-making between the interviewer and interviewee/s. Contributors to Kathryn Roulston's edited book on *Interactional Studies of Qualitative*

Research Interviews (2019b) explore the dynamics of individual and group interviews, variously exploring the identities of those involved, the conversational resources they bring and the social actions they co-produce as part of the interview. The generation of knowledge that is the interview can weave between different forms of interactional exchanges throughout an interview and the ways interviewers seek to negotiate and manage these situations as the interview unfolds. Interviewer and interviewee/s may exchange shared insider knowledge, collaborating in constructing questions and responses, for example, or they may have differing and sometimes competing perspectives and agendas, and justification, mitigation, recovery and reparation interactional work by all parties may result.

The context in which the interview takes place is also an element for interactional dynamics, with many qualitative researchers now meditating on the implications of moving from in-person to online interviewing, which we mention later and discuss further in Chapter 4. As Marnie Howlett (2021) points out, researchers have been concerned about generating meaningful conversations and managing the interactions in online interviews. For example, the video 'headshot' (where cameras are enabled) means that both interviewer and interviewee cannot fully observe each other's body language. Nonetheless, she concludes that the interactional dynamics in online research interviews 'allowed for new armchair approaches to interact with our participants' (12) and thus different knowledges.

Transformative Approaches

A transformative research paradigm, as put forward by Donna Mertens (2009), is a shift in basic beliefs that guide research to bring in the culturally diverse voices of people who are at the social margins in order to further social justice and realize social change. Transformative methodology is an overarching metaphysical framework or umbrella within which Mertens includes qualitative research that is guided by feminist, emancipatory, Indigenous, inclusive, participatory, co-production and other alternative principles of knowledge production. She argues that the various approaches have in common basic beliefs and methodological implications focusing on '(1) the tensions that arise when unequal power relationships surround the investigation of what seem to be intransigent social problems and (2) the strength found in communities when their rights are respected and honored' (11). This commonality may be the case. Equally, though, it is important not to elide approaches and obscure important and useful distinctions. So our use of the 'transformative research' heading under which we discuss, in turn, the examples of feminism, emancipatory and decolonizing/Indigenous methodologies is standing for approaches that intersect, articulate and overlap at points.

Feminisms and Interviews

There are a range of feminist approaches, including Black, intersectional, liberal, post-colonial, postmodern, psychoanalytic, queer, radical, socialist and standpoint, but what feminisms largely have in common is a focus on drawing attention to embedded gendered inequalities and power (Tong and Botts 2018). For many, their feminist perspective and feminist research are linked to a social change agenda. Feminist research has often been characterized as *qualitative* research *by* women *on* women and *for* women, but feminists also conduct quantitative research and research on men, and men can conduct research adopting feminist perspectives. Nonetheless, many feminist researchers are concerned with giving voice to women's own accounts of their understandings, experiences and interests. Feminisms have challenged conventional approaches to research and what counts as knowledge, including making major contributions to transforming how qualitative interviewing is understood (Doucet and Mauthner 2008; Golombisky 2018).

Feminist activism and scholarship about the process of qualitative interviews posed a major challenge to male-dominated, positivist ideas about the possibility and desirability of a mechanistic, unbiased, scientific, value-free and objective interview. For example, in a now-classic influential piece, Ann Oakley (1981) contended that detached, uncontaminated interviewing practice was impossible and morally indefensible, and indeed non-hierarchical engagement was a feature of generating knowledge and insight. She suggested that there can be 'no intimacy without reciprocity' (49), where researchers give back something of themselves to their participants.

Oakley's contribution stimulated a rich vein of feminist discussions about the possibilities and impossibilities of non-hierarchical relations, empathy and rapport in qualitative interviewing practice and the implications for knowledge production. Some have contended that rapport has the potential to be exploitative and in conflict with feminist aims of equitable power sharing. Some have detailed the way that systematic social divisions and characteristics, such as class, ethnicity, age, sexuality and so on, cut across gender and create power imbalances between women researchers and their subjects and restrict the ability to know the 'Other' through interviews. Others have explored interviews as a two-way flow of power relations between the researcher and the researched. And still others have questioned the extent to which there is any single, core and coherent social position and identity for both researchers and research subjects within an interview, and any single coherent knowledge to be constructed (see postmodern approaches later) (see Letherby 2003 and Thwaites 2017 for reviews of the debates).

Emancipatory Approaches and Interviews

Key motifs of emancipatory approaches are issues of power and liberation from oppression, and a central tenet is that all people should control their own lives and society generally (Freire 2018). Traditional or conventional research is regarded as inevitably political since it represents the interests of particular, usually powerful and colonizing, groups in society. The argument is that researchers cannot be independent: they are either on the side of the oppressors or the oppressed. From an emancipatory perspective, the aim of conducting research is to enable the voices of marginalized groups to be heard on their own terms – to understand the world in order to change it and achieve social justice (Humphries et al. 2000).

An emancipatory approach is concerned with the politics of research in fields of life characterized by social discrimination and marginalization, such as minority ethnic and Indigenous populations, children and older people, disabled and working-class people. The emphasis is on working collaboratively with, and placing control in the hands of, the people who are living the research topic rather than researchers. Members of the social group whose lives and circumstances form the subject of the research are viewed as co-constructors of knowledge and validators of claims to knowledge. Inclusive or participatory research, where the research is owned or led by the local or social group in question with researchers in a facilitatory role, provides a good example (Nind 2014).

Adherents of emancipatory research practice nonetheless identify several tensions and contradictions in the process. The idea of 'better' knowledge being produced through peer and participatory research can be instrumental rather than empowering. Ideas about marginalized group membership can be essentializing and ignore power relations within the group itself. And perhaps most telling, the very activity of pursuing liberation and empowerment through research involves relations of dominance, where emancipation is conferred on disempowered groups by researchers, which runs the risk of perpetuating the status quo.

Decolonization, Indigenous Knowledges and Interviews

Decolonization of knowledge highlights how the process of its conceptualization and production is not neutral and is inextricably linked with power. As Bagele Chilisa points out (2019), Euro-Western philosophies, cultures and histories provide the foundations for self-serving canons of truth, excluding and suppressing the knowledge systems of colonized, marginalized and oppressed peoples. Decolonization of research is about dismantling the embedded imperialism, distortions and erasures in dominant knowledge systems, opening up to context-dependent ways of researching and knowing beyond Western modes. There is no single Indigenous approach to knowledge production, but they have in common a foundation in connectedness, respectful and trusting relationships, responsibility and transparent accountability, and an aim to transform fundamentally the whole nature of the research endeavour and serve social justice (see Chilisa 2019; Smith 2021).

Chilisa (2019) critiques the dominant, conventional interview method as founded in asymmetrical interviewer–interviewee relations and the dominance of standard academic disciplinary theories, terms and concepts in shaping interview questions. Margaret Kovach (2019) positions the connection of a conversational method within an Indigenous approach to a deep purpose of sharing stories as a means of transmitting knowledge between individuals and groups and to assisting and being accountable to others. She notes how preparation for research using what the dominant paradigms refer to as interviews may include Western-based ideas about literature review, design of study and so on, but that with Indigenous approaches there would also be preparations that were relational, such as participating in ceremonies, and clear planning for how the research and researcher will give back to the community.

Decolonization of knowledge production and an Indigenous framework for data generation then enable interviews as a method of research to become a transformative process. While Euro-Western researchers as non-Indigenous people cannot practice Indigenous methods, they may be in alliance with them, and these approaches can at least serve as models of challenges to and alternatives for the framing of research and interviews.

Postmodernism and Interviews

Postmodernism is a broad philosophical term, extending across social science and the arts and humanities. There are various versions, but postmodern approaches share a turning away from the possibility of universal systems of thought, challenging the legitimacy of meta-narratives, such as modernist beliefs. Dichotomous distinctions between objectivity and subjectivity, fact and fiction and indeed researcher and researched are regarded as having broken down. There are no straightforward facts and meanings that can form knowledge; rather knowledge and its creation are subject to critique and negotiation, and many versions of the truth exist side by side (Scheurich 2013).

At their most radical, postmodern approaches detach representation from experience and so challenge the possibility of interviewing (or any other method) as a means of social enquiry and indeed the endeavour of social research itself. Other postmodernists still see potential and meaning in reflexive interview practice that is aware of the relationship between the means of knowledge production and social reality. Jaber Gubrium and James Holstein (2003a: 29) argue that postmodern interviews disrupt the classic technical contours of the designated interviewer–interviewee roles; they are not about the imparting of one person's or a group's world view as interviewees to another who, as researcher, will turn it into knowledge (see also Scheurich 2013). Interviews cannot refer to some objective reality beyond themselves. Rather, it is the exchange itself, between an interviewee or interviewees and an interviewer, that is of significance and meaning – when, how and why those involved ask questions, construct and tell stories about particular events and experiences in particular ways, and so on (see contributions to Gubrium and Holstein 2003b). It is in this approach that Brinkmann and Kvale's idea of the researcher as traveller is fulfilled.

Realisms and Interviews

Realisms assume the existence of a world that is independent of people's perceptions of it (echoing positivism) but regards that world as accessible only through people's subjectivity and senses, including those of researchers (echoing interpretivism). There are various versions of the approach, such as critical or scientific, but a key feature is the intention of generating causal explanations that refer to structures, mechanisms and contexts that shape people's actions and which are real but independent of our knowing them. Realists are concerned with representing the structural order of the external (material, or material and social) world that underlies the experience of it (Vandenberghe 2014). Nick Emmel (2013) puts forward five propositions about a realist methodology. To paraphrase: social reality is rich and deep and has causal effect; accounts of social reality can only be weak constructions; realist investigation moves iteratively between ideas and evidence; realist explanations attempt to work out the relation between ideas and evidence; these explanations can only be provisional and should be tested and refined through ongoing critical engagement. (See also Joseph Maxwell's (2012) introduction to using a critical realist perspective in qualitative research.)

In terms of qualitative research interviews from a realist approach, even if reality and structures are not fully available to people, researchers can still grasp it by working from interviewees' accounts of their understandings and experiences in dialogue with theories about what social reality is like and how it works. The approach also recognizes that researchers' values are inherent in all phases of the research process and that truth is negotiated through dialogue. Thus, while the objective structuring of reality cannot be comprehended in a perfect way, qualitative interviewing enables researchers to gain information that is true to participants' understandings and provides an approach that is able to create or challenge, endorse or adapt, theories. A realist approach to interviewing, then, is theory-driven. It can involve the researcher exploring with an interviewee their tentative theories about the phenomena under investigation with the aim of assembling, refining or consolidating that theory (Mukumbang et al. 2019).

Psychoanalytic Approaches and Interviews

Psychoanalytic approaches are concerned with emotion and unconscious processes at the heart of subjectivity. They share a commitment to challenging the idea of a rational, knowing subject. Rather, such approaches assume that there are levels of people's perception and experience that are both deeply irrational and difficult to access. Broadly, a psychoanalytic version of subjectivity holds that people resist certain memories, feelings or desires and repress them from conscious thought because they feel them to be bad or forbidden or they do not make sense. People are unconsciously defended against acknowledging and experiencing the ambivalence and anxiety that the internal conflict of feeling things that are deemed unacceptable brings about, through psychic mechanisms such as projection, splitting, transference, fantasy and so on (Elliott 2015).

The implications for conducting qualitative interviews taking a psychoanalytic approach are in the rejection of the idea that people are consciously self-aware and know why they think, say and do, and can report this directly to researchers (as with interpretive approaches). Researchers taking a psychoanalytic approach to interviews thus argue for the use of an unstructured narrative mode to allow room for unconscious processes to surface (a hidden psychic structuring that has some echoes of the critical realist structuring of reality), as well as multiple and inconsistent subjectivity (with resonances with postmodern understandings of personhood and knowledge). The seven aspects of enabling knowing through the psychoanalytic research interview that Brinkmann and Kvale (2015) identify, for example, include the intensive individual case study; the open and non-directive mode of interviewing; the interpretation of meaning that allows for ambiguity and contradiction; the temporal dimension intertwining past, present and future; and the human interaction involving emotions. Interest in unconscious processes is not centred on those of the interviewee alone; the subjectivity of the researcher is also implicated.

*   *   *

We have not provided exhaustive coverage of the various philosophical approaches to qualitative research but have focused on a range of ways that we can understand interviews as a means of generating knowledge about the social world. Our concern with how philosophies locate researchers and participants as speakers in interviews means that, for example, we have not looked at New Materialist philosophies. New Materialisms are centrally concerned with the materiality of the social and natural world: a post-humanism that moves research methodologies away from humanistic methods such as interviewing that focus on voices and actions (Fox and Alldred 2018). Rather, there might be a focus on the matter involved in the interview process such as the researcher body, recording technology and interview location as agentic (e.g. Marn and Wolegemuth 2017). Nonetheless, when qualitative researchers think through the implications of conducting qualitative interviews, they do so within the context of other – more prosaic and institutional – material parameters that govern and shape the research interview process.

Institutional Research Governance Procedures and Interviews

'Research governance' is a term covering a range of regulations, principles and standards that lay down what is considered good practice in research. The governance regime addresses issues such as risk assessment, health and safety, ethical conduct and so on. The institutionalization of social research regulation is often traced back to instances of bad practice in clinical research (such as taking and storing organs from dead babies without parental consent), from where the perceived need for governance expanded into social research, along with the general rise of an 'audit culture'. Research governance is said to safeguard research participants' interests and rights, protect researchers from allegations of bad practice by providing a clear framework for them to work within and promote and enhance research quality. Systems of research governance have the merit of ensuring that researchers undertake a full and reflexive consideration of the process of conducting research, thinking through the implications of their plans and practice.

Nonetheless, some qualitative researchers have been vocal in laying out what they regard as a bureaucratized ethics regulatory regime creep (e.g. Di Feliciantonio 2021). The requirement for researchers to detail a range of aspects of their research process and gain approval from a regulatory body (whether university or other institutional base) has implications for the conduct of qualitative research interviews, especially for researchers who wish to conduct interviews within emancipatory/participatory, decolonizing/Indigenous or psychoanalytic approaches. The need to (a) detail what the research is about and the tools that will be used and (b) provide written information sheets to research subjects and gain their written informed consent to participate, prior to conducting the research in order to gain approval to proceed, cuts across the community-led agenda and attempts to equalize research relationships of transformative approaches, as well as psychoanalytic narrative elicitation. Further, there is a risk that asking questions about certain, 'sensitive' subjects may be ruled out of interviews in advance by regulatory bodies, whether or not research participants want to talk about the issue. It is a mute question as to whether some of the classic social research studies, such as Whyte's study of status in gangs in the slums of Boston (*Street Corner Society* 1943/1993) or Humphreys' study of homosexual sexual behaviour in public toilets (*Tearoom Trade* 1970), would have gained ethical approval under the current research governance regime. More recently, Alice Goffman's research with a Black community in Philadelphia (*On the Run* 2014) did gain institutional ethical approval but has nonetheless received criticism as unethical (Clemens and Lincoln 2020).

Technologies and Interviews

Available technologies have long shaped the practice of qualitative interviews. Prior to the development in the 1950s of portable audio tape recorders, now followed by even lighter and smaller digital recorders for in-person interviews and inbuilt recording facilities for video calling platforms, researchers conducting interviews relied on memory and note-taking. The placement and quality of audio and video recording technologies shape how much of the linguistic and interactional nuances of the interview are picked up and later turned into written words that form transcripts that are then often uploaded into other technologies – computer-aided qualitative data analysis software (CAQDAS), to be subjected to analysis.

These various technologies shape how we understand the nature and standing of qualitative interviews, resonating with our previous discussions of the radical critique of interviews, the qualitative interviewer as miner or traveller and the various philosophical approaches to qualitative research and interviews that we have reviewed earlier. As part of his assessment of the audio recorder as the primary tool for qualitative interviews, for example, Les Back (2010) ponders whether or not a recording tool that captures participants' spoken words verbatim confines the researcher through confusing socially shaped accounts (their form) with authentic truth (their content). Back is discussing conventional in-person interviews, but the same point applies to the video and/or audio recording of online interviewing, with a surge in both the platforms and technologies available for this and their use spurred by the restrictions put in place for the Covid-19 pandemic. These mediated approaches may have wider implications too, with Marnie Howlett (2021: 5) raising the question of whether digital methods are appropriate to answer the same research questions as those for immersive in-person interactions and concluding that while online interviewing is still 'being there', it is of a different type and not necessarily suited to all types or topics of research. We follow up the process of online interviewing in Chapter 5. A challenge to the ubiquity of audio recording is the alternative of the 'slow interview', which involves taking written notes that are checked with the interviewee as the interview progresses – a technique that makes clear the constructed nature of both form and content (Young et al. 2021).

The text-based documents created from interviews, however recorded, add other layers to these debates about the standing of interview material. Transcription requires a series of underlying interpretative representational decisions in order to construct the spoken into the written, whether carried out by a human transcriber or computer software package. The resulting transcript renders the dynamic ebb and flow of the interview voices and exchanges in real time into a permanently fixed state. The nature of the conventions shaping transcription depend on research traditions, aims and interests as discussed in Alexa Hepburn and Galina Boden (2017) and Christopher Jenks (2011). From reading such texts, it will become clear to novice transcribers that a systematic set of good practice conventions for laying out the transcript, speaker identification, turn-taking and so on, is required.

The extent to which the sharing and reuse of transcripts through research data archives at least in part provide the implicit philosophical ground for researchers practising qualitative interviews has been discussed (Mauthner and Parry 2009), keying into the 'interviewer as miner' aspect of the radical critique of interviews debate. Subsequently, the CAQDAS that facilitates the analysis of transcribed qualitative interview texts, as well as graphics, audio and visual material, raises similar tensions about what this means for conceptions of the nature of interviews as they become 'fixed' as fact in electronic files, existing as a reality outside of the context of their production, potentially available as a product independent to the interaction and people that produced them (see also Chapter 8).

In the chapters that follow, we go on to explore and reflect on the forms, settings, tools and practices of the interview mode of knowledge production.

CHAPTER 3

Forms That Qualitative Interviews Can Take

Introduction

In this chapter, we cover a variety of forms of interviews, including ethnographic interviews, a range of biographical and narrative approaches and challenges to dominant interview methods from Indigenous and cross-cultural perspectives. Throughout our discussion, we link these forms to the broad philosophical positions underlying their use. We also consider interviewing people in groups and couples as well as mixing or combining interviews with other, qualitative, quantitative and arts-based methods.

General Forms of Qualitative Interviews

The major forms of qualitative interviews are semi- and unstructured interviews. In a typical semi-structured interview, the researcher has a list of questions or series of topics they want to cover in the interview, an interview guide (see Chapter 5 for examples), but there is flexibility in how and when the questions are put and how the interviewee can respond. The interviewer can probe answers, pursuing a line of discussion opened up by the interviewee, and a dialogue can ensue. In general, the interviewer is interested in the context and content of the interview, how the interviewee understands the topic(s) under discussion and what they want to convey to the interviewer. Basically, these interviews allow much more space for interviewees to answer on their own terms than structured interviews but do provide some structure for comparison across interviewees in a study by covering the same topics, even in some instances asking some questions of all participants in the same format.

In the unstructured interview, the researcher has aims for the research and a topic of study, but the importance of the method is to allow the interviewee to talk from their own perspective using their own frame of reference and ideas and meanings that are familiar to them. Flexibility is the key, with the researcher able to respond to the interviewee, to trace the meaning that he or she attaches to what has been characterized as a 'conversation with a purpose' (Burgess 1984: 102) and to develop unexpected themes and adjust the content of interviews and possibly emphasis of the research as a result of issues that emerge in any interview. The researcher can have an aide-memoire to remind them of areas into which to lead the conversation (see Chapter 5). Or they can use a single question to begin the interview, where the interviewee is prompted to embark on their story. The latter can be the case in some psychological or psycho-socially oriented interviews and in some oral history or biographical approaches. Flexibility is key to the unstructured interview, and phenomenological philosophical approaches underlie the method – constructivism, symbolic interactionism and ethnomethodology.

Both semi- and unstructured interviews are qualitative methods in use across the social sciences. The form of the interview might be similar, or even the same; what will differ are the particular theoretical positions and concomitant approaches to analysis and interpretation adopted by the researcher from their philosophical and possibly disciplinary perspective.

Specific Forms of Qualitative Interviews

The Ethnographic Interview

Ethnography is the basic qualitative method deriving from early twentieth-century anthropology, although now widely used in many other social science disciplines. Ethnography is itself constructed from multiple qualitative methods, including observation and participant observation, and can incorporate the collection of demographic and other statistical data about the researched as appropriate (see discussion of mixed methods later). Critically, however, ethnography involves social exploration, protracted investigation, spending time in the site of study in person or via the internet and the interpretation of local and situated cultures based on paying attention to the singular and concrete (Hammersley and Atkinson 2019). Interviews are clearly important, initially perhaps with a key informant who can provide crucial information about the individuals, groups and social relations within the chosen research setting. Key informants have a formal or informal position that gives them specialist knowledge about the people and processes that are the subject of research (such as preacher, head of department, community leader and oldest club member). Interviews with key informants can help illuminate situations, behaviours and attitudes that researchers otherwise could not access or understand. But equally key informants may mislead the researcher or withhold knowledge in interviews.

Interviews in the field can be formal (perhaps recorded, perhaps using an interview guide) or informal, as and when an appropriate situation, person or group becomes available. In this instance, flexibility, practice in recall and making notes after the event become key researcher/interviewing skills. It is possible to use a small unobtrusive audio recorder in some informal settings, such as a mobile phone, depending on the relationship with the participants and the types of setting. The term 'ethnographic interview' has been used in a way akin to 'qualitative, unstructured interview' (see James Spradley's classic *The Ethnography Interview*, 1979), particularly given the time and economic constraints on protracted periods of research immersion.

Eliciting the Interviewee's Own Story

One set of forms of interviews is specifically designed to elicit a story, their own story from the participants in the research, with particular inflections from the originating stance of the research.

These are oral history, life course, life history, biographical and narrative interviews.

Oral history draws its methods from history and sociology and emphasizes the importance of time and memory, and people are interviewed about their past experiences. Oral historians also tend to try to give expression to marginalized voices, particularly in relation to class, gender and ethnicity (e.g. Chansky et al. 2021). Paul Thompson makes a distinction between oral history, which for him is focused on the past, and life history, which is focused on the present and can cover the whole life (Thompson with Bornat 2017). From this perspective, in oral history approaches, the focus of enquiry and the question(s) facilitating talk in the interview could relate to the interviewee's life experiences of a particular historical event or period, for example, the Second World War, 9/11 and the Covid-19 pandemic, or to a particular biographical life event. This event could be their earliest memory or the birth of their first child, for example. In life history, the focus and facilitating question(s) could be more wide ranging, covering various aspects of their life (work, family and home). The question(s) could open up the possibility of the interviewee telling their whole life story in their own words. In some versions of this approach, the aim is to elicit this story, which could be seen as an autobiography, with the researcher staying very much out of the picture after the initial question or prompt. In each of these types of interviews, points can be followed up with supplementary questions if necessary or to clarify the meaning of what is being said if there is any doubt, and both versions can be combined with other sources of data such as documents – diaries, photographs, letters and so on (see Chapter 5).

Bringing the *life course* into consideration in these biographical approaches draws attention to normative expectations that can constrain or enable individuals at particular stages of life, the effects of biological ageing and cohort effects of being members of a particular generation. For example, in the United States, the generation born between 1901 and 1927 is known as the Greatest Generation, with lives and experiences shaped by the Great Depression and participation in the Second World War, while in both the United States and the United Kingdom, the post-1945 baby boomers have been characterized as living through a time of affluence and optimism, and children of Indigenous Australians forcibly removed from their families over the twentieth century are referred to as the Stolen Generations. All of these elements, normative expectations, biological ageing and cohort effects will interact, affecting the individual life as both lived and told, and could be the focus of attention, or at least consideration, in designing a study using life history and biographical methods. They can also play a part in analysis, interpretation and understanding.

The analytical *life history* method was pioneered by W. I. Thomas and Florian Znaniecki, exemplified by an autobiography written for them by a Polish immigrant to the United States and taken forward in a series of powerful studies of the life histories of 'everyday people' by the Chicago School of sociologists in the first half of the twentieth century (Tierney and Lanford 2019). From this perspective, the purpose of the individual life history was to draw subjective aspects of experience into an understanding of the social. Although 'life history' and 'life story' are sometimes used interchangeably, Robert Miller (2000) suggests that in the history of the method, an early distinction was made between life story as an account of their life given by one individual and life history where other sources, including newspaper reports and public records, could validate the individual account. This confirmation or validation through external sources (triangulation) can be seen as related to the positivist modes of social enquiry, which swept into a dominant position in sociology in the 1950s. In this period, qualitative and biographical methods became submerged.

A resurgence of life history interviews ensued in the 1970s, especially in Europe, drawing on the influential work of C. Wright Mills, who was concerned with the interplay between personal biography, history and society, and argued that 'neither the life of an individual nor the history of a society can be understood without understanding both' (Mills 1959: 3). Contemporary life histories have often focused on giving voice to marginalized people and also challenging assumptions about homogenous and linear time life histories in contemporary lives (Tierney and Lanford 2019). A turn to biographical methods has been suggested (Chamberlayne et al. 2000), where life history interviews that pursue aspects of an individual's biography have become used more widely in the social sciences. In most cases, one aspect of the biography might be sought, for example, experience of childbirth, of family life, of health or perhaps educational or career trajectories. The focus might be quite tight, for example, experiences of a particular type of educational scheme or institution. William Tierney and colleagues, for example, draw on the life histories of four lower-caste, male Indian adolescents to examine the societal factors that hinder success both during and after university studies (2019). Whatever the topic of the research, the principles of the interview will be the same, and depend on the underlying approach, but the practice might vary.

A type of *biographical interview* is employed in the Biographic-Narrative Interpretive Method (BNIM), drawing on the German life history interview methodology of hermeneutic reconstruction (Chamberlayne et al. 2000; Wengraf 2008). Here a single question is aimed to induce a non-interrupted narrative from the interviewee, with the interviewer making as little intrusion as possible into the story. The researchers who developed this method take a phenomenological approach to understanding biographical data, focusing on the individual's perspective within a knowable historical and structural context, that is, some external (historical/social) facts of their life can be known, and have developed a specific analytic process to be used for this particular type of interview (Rosenthal 2018; Wengraf 2008). Christina Peta and colleagues (2019) argue that the BNIM interviewing techniques facilitate the voice of marginalized minority groups and illustrate this in relation to a study of disabled women in Zimbabwe.

From an interpretivist perspective, the *narrative interview* is based on the idea that people produce stories about themselves and their identities through time that draw not only on their own experiences and understanding but on culturally circulating stories that help them interpret and make sense of the world and themselves within it. Communities, social groups and individuals tell stories conveying meanings that are specific to their experiences and ways of life. Narrative interviewing builds on this awareness of the role that storytelling plays in the social world, to elicit rich temporal stories from interviewees about some aspect of their life. As with the BNIM, the narrative interviewer aims to enable the interviewee to tell their own story in their own words in their own way through an initial open and straightforward question that will elicit an extended account. But narrative interviewers also recognize that the story told is a retrospective construction generated by the interviewee in the context of the interview and for the interviewer as an audience (Andrews 2021). Catherine Reissman sums up the narrative interview as a conversation where interviewees can develop narrative accounts; speaker and listener/questioner render events and experiences meaningfully – collaboratively. The model of a 'facilitating' interviewer who asks questions, and a vessel-like respondent who gives answers, is replaced by two active *participants* who jointly construct narrative and meaning. (2007: 23, original emphasis)

For some this means that the narrative interview actively produces interactive and fluidly constructed accounts, contingent to the research encounter (Holstein and Gubrium 2016). For others, there can be embedded 'kernels' of narrative stabilities in interviewees' accounts over time, as Paul Atkinson and Cathy Sampson (2019) demonstrate from their analysis of narrative interviews, conducted fifteen years apart, with the same members of a genetics research group. These fluid/stable positions are relevant to the radical critique of interview debate we introduced in Chapter 1.

The *problem-centred interview* engages us further with the radical critique debate about the generation of interview accounts as form (co-production) or content (access to experience). The problem-centred method emphasizes both the reconstruction of knowledge about a socially relevant issue from the perspective of the interviewee and a dialogic approach of active communication between interviewer and interviewee. It has roots in the German tradition of qualitative research, is defined as a discursive-dialogic method and positions the interviewer as a 'well-informed traveller' (resonating with Brinkman and Kvale's metaphor – see Chapter 2) and the interviewee as holding everyday practical knowledge (Weitzel and Reiter 2012: 10). The method for the interview involves specific interview techniques, of open-ended elicitation of narratives in the first phase and general and specific follow-up questions in the second. (Asking questions in interviews is addressed in Chapter 5.)

The researcher moves from a direct shaper of an interview encounter to a background influence in the *self-interview* method (Keightley et al. 2012). Research participants are given a guidance sheet providing details on conducting a self-interview and some research questions to think about and asked to record themselves responding to the questions and to related objects and media, such as photographs and music, in their own time. The self-interview recording is then returned to the researcher. The benefits are said to be that 'self-interviewers' are able to pause and reflect without the discursive demands and expectations of the conventional qualitative interview.

All of the approaches discussed here can be seen as eliciting a narrative from the interviewee, and the particular choice of interview type will relate to the aims and underlying framework of the research as delineated earlier, although in the literature there can be some blurring of terms. The participation of the researcher can also vary. They can largely stand apart metaphorically, encouraging the interviewee to tell their story uninterrupted as in the BNIM method, or physically as in the self-interview. Or they can firmly regard themselves and the participant as co-producers of the interview account as with some narrative interview practitioners, or as positioned between the two in some way, as with the problem-centred interviewer and some narrative interviewers. The forms of interviews discussed here understand the interview as giving some level or kind of access to the social/historical as well as to the individual, and also to the cultural. Considering cultures can lead to questioning of researcher assumptions but also to challenges to the whole notion of the nature of an interview.

Cross-cultural interviews concern cultural divides – modes of generating meaning and communication orders – between researchers and research participants. The term can refer to an interviewer from one national context interviewing in another national context or to interviewing across sociocultural settings or sub-populations within one national context. In both cases cross-cultural interviews bring together interviewers and interviewees from different backgrounds, communicating across different culturally situated understandings and working across different racial or ethnic positionings as well perhaps as languages. In the latter case, an interpreter may be required for an interview to take place, and in cross-cultural research, generally cultural advisors or brokers can be involved. The cultural context shapes not just different substantive cultural knowledges and assumptions but also the culturally situated understandings and negotiations of sharing information and power dynamics that play out in interviews (Griffin 2018).

Taking this further, *Indigenous interviews* – or rather, interviews within Indigenous methodologies and epistemologies – challenge Western dominant modes of understanding interviewing as a method of generating research information. An Indigenous paradigm involves a far more radical step outside of conventional parameters, in quite different knowledge systems where 'research', 'research methods' and 'interviews' are not the starting point of understanding, as we discussed in Chapter 2. Interviews conducted within Western modes of research are a different endeavour from what seems to be the same process of data creation enacted within an Indigenous methodological approach. Amy-Louise Byrne and colleagues (2021) discuss cross-cultural research within a post-colonial context, where non-Indigenous researchers attempt to adopt an Indigenous conversational method, 'yarning', as an Indigenous-inspired interview technique in research with Indigenous peoples. Yarning derives from the Indigenous two-way process of exchanging meaning and explanation through storytelling and is subject to various protocols. Social yarning often happens at the start of a research interview, with interviewer and interviewee each establishing connection to physical and spiritual place as a basis for trust in exchanging knowledge. Research yarning may then occur in what can seem a circuitous fashion from non-Indigenous interview expectations, also involving a range of other forms of yarn exchange. Byrne and colleagues highlight the radically different expectations and post-colonial tensions between non-Indigenous researchers and Indigenous participants in how relationships shape information giving in interviews.

An underlying assumption in our discussion of various interview forms so far may be that we are referring to a researcher interviewing individual research participants. Interviews, however, can take place with more than one interviewee.

Interviewing Groups and Couples

The term 'group interview' can be used generically to describe any interview in which a group of people take part but can be differentiated from the *focus group* interview. Many definitions of focus groups exist in the literature, but essentially they involve a small group of people engaging in collective discussion of a topic previously selected by the researcher. With their origins in market research, as a research technique in social science, focus groups have elicited a range of criticisms and gone in and out of fashion (Morgan 1997; Morgan 2018). Among advocates, appropriate group numbers can range widely and will depend on the nature of the study and the specific situation of the group, but six to ten is often suggested in the literature. Typically the researcher moderates or runs the discussion, with a series of questions to guide its course. But a stimulus can provide a focus or starting point, for example, a photograph, film, vignette or game. If resources allow, a second researcher can be present making notes on the interactions and identifying speakers as an aid to transcription and recognition of the participant in the recording, but this is less pressing where videoing of focus groups has become more common (Stewart and Shamdasani 2017), especially with the recent major move onto online platforms in a pandemic (discussed further in Chapter 4).

The construction of focus groups is guided by the topic of research and research questions. They could be, for example, people at the same or different levels in the organization/s under study, such as schools or a business; people of the same age, class and gender; people of varying ages, classes and gender depending on the issue under study; or social groups such as members of a club or a sub-culture. So participants in the group discussion might know each other or know some or none of the others in the focus group. The groups for Rachel Ayrton's (2019) study of national identity within the South Sudanese diaspora were recruited through a community association, for example, and knew each other. Particular emphasis has been placed on the interaction taking place between the participants, the group dynamics and the insight and data that this can produce (Kitzinger 2005). Ayrton shows how the micro-dynamics of power in interactions in her focus groups were infused by and manifested wider relations of power, providing her with valuable insights into the relational significance of her substantive topic.

Focus groups can be used alone, or in conjunction with other methods, often individual interviews. Focus groups can be used at the start of a project, for generating ideas about the participants under research, since their interaction can give insight into participants' world view, the language they use and their values and beliefs about a particular issue or topic, useful in the design of the study. They can be used at the end, to get feedback on results or for assessment in an evaluation design. The rapidity with which data can be generated in focus (and other) groups is valued, but the logistical and practical issues of organizing focus groups should not be overlooked, even when the participants might all be in one organization or location. These are issues whether the focus groups are organized in person or online (Stewart and Shamdasani 2017).

Focus group interviews might be assumed to be more appropriate for non-sensitive, low-involvement topics, but many argue for their value in just such contexts, and they have been widely used for example in studying sensitive or difficult topics. This is illustrated by the use of focus groups in studies with parents and young people about the Arkansas high school sexuality education curriculum (Marshall et al. 2020) and of barriers and facilitators for help-seeking behaviour among men experiencing sexual violence (Donne et al. 2017).

Focus group interviews can then be a useful method in a range of contexts. As ever, the decision to use the method is dependent on its appropriateness for the particular piece of research, its theoretical and philosophical approach and research questions. We have suggested that the focus group is particularly valuable in giving access to social interaction, and *couple interviews* (sometimes referred to as dyads) offer access to a very particular type of interaction between two people. The general form for this joint interview is when one researcher interviews two participants who usually know each other in some way. This can happen when the interviewee asks for another person to be present, perhaps a friend or family member. It can also be appropriate in studies of illness and disability, involving a carer and the care recipient. Joint interviews can also happen unexpectedly, where perhaps someone in the setting intrudes upon the interview and stays (a parent when a child is being interviewed, a housemate when another resident in a shared house is the interviewee). A more specific and planned version involves two people in a couple relationship.

There is some debate as to whether couples should be interviewed separately or together, largely underpinned by positivist as against interpretivist positions. From an interpretivist view, interview data is dependent on the context in which it is generated, so individual and couple interviews will each provide a different perspective (Lawton 2018). Couple interviews allow a relational understanding of how a situation or relationship is experienced and negotiated, and interviewing couples in a partner relationship is enlightening on a number of levels. Rachele Bezzini (2017) argues that the relationship between the two interviewees means that joint couple interviews provide rich data, characterized by three dimensions: (i) performance, with observational data through the couples' interactions; (ii) meta-communication, with an opportunity to display the couple and family history to a multiple audience of the interviewer and their partner; and (iii) positionality, taking account of the intersection between participants' and researcher's positionalities in the wider social structure.

Mixing Qualitative Interviewing with Other Methods and Modes

The most usual mixing referred to in the context of social research is the mixing of *quantitative and qualitative methods*, and we can see from our earlier discussions that this could raise issues about incompatibility of the underpinning philosophy of these approaches. These issues have indeed provided the basis for continuing debate, with heightened interest in recent decades with the growth of an explicit mixed methods methodological field (Hesse-Biber 2015). Nonetheless, it can be pragmatic or technical rather than philosophical assumptions that drive much research in practice, and even when researchers plan to choose methods in line with the framing of a particular research question and its philosophical assumptions, in practice this might not occur. In mixing across paradigms, there has been considerable discussion about the weighting and sequence given to the qualitative or quantitative elements in mixed methods studies (Walker and Baxter 2019). There are arguments for the importance of a qualitatively informed logic of explanation for theoretically driven mixed methods research (Hesse-Biber et al. 2015; Mason 2006; Morse 2015), viewing qualitative thinking as a useful starting point for thinking outside the box and as providing critical insights into meaning and process.

Sharlene Hesse-Biber and colleagues (2015) list a number of ways that qualitatively driven researchers can design mixed methods studies, where the quantitative work is in the service of the qualitative approach, and provide examples. These include a study of rape myths among college student athletes with a sequential design, where an initial attitudinal survey was followed by focus groups and individual interviews, which revealed subjugated knowledge below the survey attitudes; in contrast to a mixed methods design about gender inequality in *Wall Street* that nested quantitative closed-ended questions about wages, career conditions and so on into a primarily qualitative in-depth interview about interpersonal and organizational dynamics.

Further, there are discussions of mixed methods as a research strategy that can transcend or subvert the qualitative–quantitative divide (Pearce 2015). Challenging ideas about paradigms and priorities, Pat Bazeley points out that qualitative and quantitative approaches are an artificial divide when 'the meaning of everything, including numbers, is theory based and all research is interpretive' (2018: 334).

While mixed methods approach often is thought of as bringing together qualitative and quantitative approaches, it is also possible to mix qualitative methods. Qualitative studies very often combine several qualitative methods, and ethnography is a typical case in this regard. This mixing will very often involve qualitative interviews with other types of qualitative methods, life history or different versions of narrative interviews combined with documentary analysis for example. Different types of interviews can be used in the same study, individual interviews combined with focus groups, in person with remote interviews, interviews with observation and all combined with different types of documentary and archival data. Liz McDonnell and colleagues' study of asexual identities (2016), for example, brought together an adapted version of the Biographic-Narrative Interpretive Method and daily diaries collecting open responses to three daily questions over time to facilitate different understandings of how people comprehend and narrate their lives.

This sort of combination represents a *multimodal* approach in mixing qualitative interviews with other methods. Multimodal research involves a range of different forms of communication modes – aural, visual and/or written, amalgamating diverse communication forms in order to make meaning on a research topic. In terms of our focus in this book, interviews can be mixed with textual, visual and creative materials, such as the various tools to engage interviewees and elicit their stories that we will discuss in Chapter 5. Roberto Santo de Roock (2019), for example, conducted an eight-month video ethnography in a US classroom encompassing participant observation, written fieldnotes, video of activities and interactions, and collecting written classwork, along with informal and formal interviews with individuals and groups. Creative methods can involve arts-based approaches using various expressive media as part of multi-modality or as part of what may be termed 'aesthetic interviews'. Torill Vist (2018) refers to 'aesthetic interviews' to denote the arts-based research encounters she had with young children in a Norwegian day care centre that drew on interpretive qualitative interview philosophies often involving music-making. Good introductions to multimodal research generally can be found in Carey Jewitt and colleagues (2016) and John Bateman and colleagues (2017).

Conclusion

In this chapter, we have introduced the general types of qualitative interviews and detailed a range of specific forms of qualitative interviews that elicit the interviewees' own stories, including biographies and narratives, as well as cross-cultural, linking them to their philosophical grounding. We have considered interviewing groups and couples as well as individuals, and we have discussed the qualitative interview in the context of mixing methods, multimodal and arts-based methods. In the following chapter, we build on the discussion of types of interviews here to think about the different contexts in which any of them might occur, with particular reference to space and place.

CHAPTER 4

Where Qualitative Interviews Take Place

Introduction

In Chapter 3 we discussed forms that the qualitative interview can take. Here we discuss further types of interviews, focusing on and considering the implications of the setting for the type of interaction that takes place and the data that can be generated. We examine the importance of various settings for in-person interviews and 'walking and talking' interviews. The discussion continues with interviews where the researcher and researched are in different places: email interviews and self-interviews where the researcher is not present at the same time as the participant, and methods where they are co-present in time but not in place: messaging, telephone and interviewing via videoconferencing platforms – the latter being a practice that gained ground in response to the Covid-19 pandemic.

In-person Interview Settings

Earlier we have discussed pragmatic approaches to issues of research methodology and methods, and a pragmatic approach to the location of in-person interviews (as might be advocated in textbooks) would suggest finding a space that is available for use, convenient and accessible to participants and researchers, where you could avoid interruption and make an adequate sound recording of the conversation. Any experienced researcher will smile at this point, thinking of the places and spaces in which they have undertaken interviews, some of which probably met none of these criteria. Privacy might be an issue and so a private rather than a public space is more suitable, the home of the researched possibly, bringing its own concerns and complications. But private rooms can be available in otherwise public spaces, the researcher's office in a university or the office of the participant in an organization of which they are part. We can see that just naming these potential settings for an interview further complicates an already complex situation in relation to the power and positionality (their social status and identity) of the researcher and researched in a range of hierarchies (see also Chapter 7).

Positions in hierarchies of gender, class, age, ethnicity and other dimensions are not just aspects of the multiple identities of individuals (or groups) but are experienced, created and enacted in *places*. Think of a school, redolent of power hierarchies; a researcher accessing children in school has multiple levels of power and control to negotiate, and once in contact with the children the adult–child power relationship itself colours the interaction. It is hard for a child or young person interviewed in a school setting not to see the researcher as a teacher, or allied with teachers/adults in this context. On their part, teachers and other powerful figures can undermine the confidentiality offered to children, expecting access to any information gathered. But homes too have their own micro-geographies and sets of familial power relations, and spaces in homes available for research vary considerably with the social positioning of the participants. It can be argued that the public permeates the private, and the domestic space often is linked to public space through the internet in a two-way process through various social media.

Micro-geographies of Interview Sites

Often researchers offer the choice of setting to the interviewee, who might like to meet in a public place in which they are comfortable – a café, a pub or a park. Noise affecting the recording, being able to hear what each other says adequately, and privacy are practical considerations here. These can also apply to workplaces of different types: factories, a prison, an open-plan office and a school staffroom. If other people are within hearing distance or can enter the space where the interview takes place, this can create tension for both interviewer and interviewee and affect how and what can be discussed. When undertaking research in different institutions and organizations, the researcher may be facilitated by the provision of a suitable room or left to take their chances in whatever spaces are available.

Many researchers have noted that space and place are active elements in the interview, with the location being both a physical or indeed virtual 'space' and a 'place' where identities and power dynamics unfold in various ways. The interview site itself produces 'micro-geographies' of socio-spatial relations and meaning that reflect the relationships of the researcher with the participant, the participant with the site, and the site within a broader sociocultural and power context that affects both the researcher and the participant. Marilou Gagnon, Jean Jacob and Janet McCabe (2015) compare their various experiences of interviewing in a range of health institutions, community-based organizations, academic offices and home settings, arguing that certain questions are easier or more difficult to ask and to answer related to the nature of the space and place involved, while Hanna Herzog (2012) discusses her experience of interviewing Palestinian Arab women, where the women's selection of interview location was shaped by and expressed their social and political position rooted in inequality between Arabs and Jews in Israel and between men and women generally and in Palestinian society specifically. The social meaning of the space and place of the interview was constituted, negotiated and contested in the interview process.

At the pragmatic level, as researchers we do desire a room where we can speak privately to the research participant(s). Many researchers have also pointed out that the interview site, in all its messiness and social embeddedness, is a source of information and data beyond that generated in the interview. Seeing the participant in context (in their home, their classroom and their workplace), surrounded by the material culture of their created space, and possibly interacting with others in that space, offers a wealth of information beyond that obtained, and possibly obtainable, in an interview, providing an ethnographic dimension to the exchange.

A further type of interview builds on the access that space and place can provide researchers to the lives, identities, biographies and memories of participants. The walking interview takes place in the participant's environment.

Walking and Talking

As with many methods and types of qualitative interview, the walking interview and the mobile or go-along method have their roots in ethnography in the generic practice of 'hanging out'. For the walking interview, participants are accompanied on an outing, rooted in everyday routines with the researcher asking questions, listening and observing, and exploring the participant's practices and experiences as they move through and interact with their physical and social environment. Mobile or go-along interviews can similarly be accomplished on foot but also through other modes of transit, including bicycle, car and public transport. In Jessica Finlay and Jay Bowman's mobile interviews with older people (2017), some walked unaided or with a walking aid, while others used a wheelchair or motorized scooter. Technological advances in video and cameras, tablets, smartphones and digital records (see Chapter 2) enable researchers to record, share and transmit audio and visual materials generated in walking interviews. The length of time and tempo for the walk or go-along may depend on the type of questions asked and depth of discussion, as well as interviewee and researcher abilities.

To engage in a walking interview is to 'follow' someone on a walk that may be part of their routine activity, or a route that they have chosen because it has some special meaning for them or is a new discovery, dependent on the focus of the research. The interview proceeds as the researcher and interviewee walk, talking along the way, and they share the embodied physical and mental experiences of sights, sounds and smells as they pass through the social and material surroundings of streets, buildings, greenery, the weather and other people:

A strength of the walking interview is that the social conditions are laid bare and their relevance in the research process: the orality, landscape, the sense-scape (sound, smell, touch, visual), perceptions and emotions are based within context, within which both interviewer and interviewee interact. (O'Neill and Roberts 2020)

In this multisensory richness, the walking interview connects with multimodal methods discussed in Chapter 3.

Finlay and Bowman (2017), from a social geography point of view, suggest five strengths of mobile interviews: (i) generating spatially grounded and place-specific data, (ii) access to subtle and complex meanings of place, (iii) opportunities for flexible and collaborative interaction with participants in situ, (iv) building of rapport and adjustment of participant–researcher power dynamics, and (v) generation of rich (geographic) data. They also note some of the practical and safe preparation steps, including carrying mobile phones with location services during the fieldwork, carrying water and snacks and bringing appropriate clothing.

We have discussed the importance and potential effects of in-person settings in qualitative interviews. There are also interviews in which the researcher and participant are not in the same physical location – increasingly a method of adoption and topic of discussion in response to the Covid-19 pandemic.

Together and Apart in Time and Space

In this section we discuss types of interviews where researcher and participant are separated in time and space. They might be in different time zones or separate locations at any distance apart. They could be responding to each other *asynchronically* via email or provision of data collection guidelines for self-interviews. Or they may be communicating *synchronically* using text via messaging apps, through voice using telephonic communication or – a major growth area in qualitative social research – through the use of videoconferencing platforms. Janet Salmons (2015) provides a useful extended discussion of various forms of online interviews. Here we provide an overview and draw on lessons from the recent increased uptake of the possibilities.

Asynchronous: Email and Self-interviews

In an *email interview*, the participants can be widely geographically separated, including worldwide. As with all types of qualitative interviews, the email interview must produce data appropriate for your research questions, and participants need to be comfortable writing about their experiences. While an email exchange can be quite rapid, when using email for qualitative interviews, it is more likely that the exchanges will be asynchronous, with gaps of varying length between them. There are numerous advantages of the technique: it is written, producing text, obviating the need for transcription and saving time and resources, although this might lead to a less spontaneous account than produced in other interview methods. It can enable the inclusion of participants who would not otherwise be able to participate in the research, such as disability and/or time pressures. The spatial separation might be advantageous, reducing the possibility of embarrassment for the participant and less obtrusive. The email interview offers considerable flexibility about when it takes place, with the participant in control of the flow, their response triggering the next communication from the researcher. The researcher can have several interviews running at the same time, and both researcher and participant can have time for reflection on the responses and on the future direction of the research: 'offering the researcher a way to strategically work with the extended time frame that comes with asynchronous interviewing . . . a strategy that utilises open-ended introductory questions, follow-up questions, and cross-fertilization of multiple interviews carried out simultaneously' (Dahlin 2021: 2). Skills in interviewing by email include attention to timing the flow of questions and judging how the interview is progressing where it can be hard to assess the meaning of time gaps. In general, it is better not to send all of the questions at once (although an indicative list of topics or issues sent early is useful) but to send them in the form of dialogue and exchange.

In the *self-interview*, the researcher is physically absent from the interview site, and the interviewee undertakes the interview in their own way in their own space. Emma Keightley and colleagues developed the 'self-interview' to use in the empirical study of memory, drawing on oral history approaches (Keightley et al. 2012). When piloting their study of practices of remembering, particularly about the 'life cycle' and stages in it, their participants associated photography and recorded music with memory and remembering. Initially using in-person interviews, the researchers realized that the participants needed more time to think and to reflect on the memories elicited. They asked potential informants to record themselves talking about photos and recorded music and how these operated as vehicles of memory in their lives. The participants were provided with a guide sheet including the areas to be covered. Removing the interviewer enabled the participants to pause, think and reflect on their chosen images and possibly to come to terms with any emotions evoked, choosing when to talk and for how long at any time. For these researchers self-interviews can capture the cross-temporal relation between the present in which the participants are remembering and the remembered past, exploring how the past is made sense of in the present. There are also suggestions that some reflective autoethnographic practices are akin to self-interviews (Crawley 2012).

Audio diaries, where the participant can record their thoughts about their experiences as they occur, may be thought of as a form of self-interview. They similarly are without the direct mediating presence of the researcher, albeit the researcher of course is guiding the research. Marci Cottingham and Rebecca Erickson assert that digital recorders are 'innocuous gadgets that are small, easy to use, and transportable' (2020: 561). Based on their study of the emotional experiences and management practices of US healthcare workers, where they asked nurses to reflect on how they felt during and after their shift, who and what influenced their emotions and how they responded to their emotions or the emotions of others, in daily digital voice recordings, they argue that audio diaries can provide a window into spontaneous emotions as they occur.

Synchronous Text and Voice: Messaging, Telephone and Video

Synchronous but remote interview methods can involve text, audio and audio-visual communication. These rapidly developing modes of contact are expanding the scope and range of qualitative interviews.

Instant messaging apps, for example Messenger, Snapchat, Telegram, WeChat and WhatsApp, often are part of people's everyday mobile social connectivity. As such they can prove a flexible and discrete interview mode for researchers seeking to gain insights into phenomena that may otherwise be hard to access. Katja Kaufmann and colleagues argue that using instant messaging is best suited for interviews focusing on what participants are doing, where and how, in real time, within the places and spaces in which they are embedded, and can be used as part of multimodal research:

> On an agreed day, the researcher repeatedly asks questions, depending on the focus, for example, 'What are you doing right now?' 'Where are you right now?' 'What meaning does the situation/space you are in have for you?' in a private messenger chat to start a conversation. Once the participant has replied, the researcher can dive deeper into the situation with further inquiries to learn more about the specificities of the participant's momentary experience as well as their social, physical and affective-emotional situatedness and embeddedness. The researcher can also ask the participant for multimodal materials that elaborate the situation. (Kaufmann et al. 2021: 3)

As well as individual exchanges, instant messaging apps can be used to undertake group interviews. Julienne Chen and Pearlyn Neo (2019) conducted focus groups with up to five participants for their research project on waste management and household item reuse in Singapore via WhatsApp. In this case, they spread out activities and topics for discussion over a five-day period to take advantage of the app as an intermittent chatting device. As with asynchronous text-based methods, instant messaging interview questions need to be phrased carefully: brief, clear, precise and requiring elaboration and explanation in answer (see Chapter 5 on asking interview questions). Other issues include not knowing if you are undertaking your interview at a convenient point or the extent to which the interviewee is engaged with your questions with no visible or audible social context cues and the levels of digital fluency among research participants.

Telephone interviews are often overlooked as an interviewing model. They can be conducted by landline or mobile and are a feasible option for researchers who are working in remote regions and/or with participants who are located in difficult places and those who are digitally disadvantaged. The benefits and drawbacks of interviews by telephone reflect many of those for instant messaging, including cost-effectiveness and convenience but lacking in contextual cues. However, tone of voice is indicative and phone interviews can enable a feeling of conversational connection combined with relative anonymity for discussing sensitive or difficult topics. Those using telephone interviews conclude that they can lead to greater articulation from both researcher and participant in the exchanges, producing rich narrative data. Kerk Kee and Andrew Schrock (2019) found telephone interviews to be a flexible and effective means of generating rich data for their studies of practices, networks and biographies in cyberinfrastructure communities, as did Laurie Drabble and colleagues (2016) for their study of women's hazardous alcohol use, while Anna Tarrant and colleagues (2021) found that the young fathers they were interviewing preferred talking about their precarious lives over the telephone. These authors stress the importance of setting up the interview as well as cultivating rapport during it.

Synchronous Voice and Image: Video Platforms

The use of videoconferencing platforms, such as Zoom, Teams, FaceTime, Skype and WhatsApp, grew exponentially during the Covid-19 pandemic and they now have become a commonplace mode of communication in everyday social life and employment and for qualitative interviews with individuals and groups. The idea that in-person interviews are the 'gold standard' has been overturned by the rich accounts produced by qualitative interview-based studies using remote digital mediation.

Strengths of video interviews include that interviewers and interviewees can see each other and pick up on (at least some) visual as well as verbal cues. There are also glimpses of interviewee's location or locations as they may move around, for example, from room to room or while walking outside (albeit the interviewee similarly has glimpses of the researcher's environment) (Howlett 2021). There are also advantages of being able to include people from a wider geographical spread, cutting costs of both time and money for researchers and participants (and with environmental benefits concerning travel). Interviewees can feel relaxed in their setting, and more power lies with them as they can pause the interview and switch off camera and microphone or log off at any time. This may mean that videoconferencing can be a good choice for sensitive topics. But there are also challenges. There can be technical difficulties, with internet going down or buffering and sound delays and cameras being unable to function: 'can you hear me?', 'I can't see you' and 'can you unmute yourself?' become a regular part of interview parlance, but may serve as part of building rapport as well as a practical function. There are also drawbacks to the interview process, where the researcher is not aware that an interviewee is unable to talk confidentially in their environment or the researcher feeling distanced in ability to respond to any distress expressed by interviewees (see review in Thunberg and Arnell (2021)). Overall though, it seems that qualitative interviewers experience videoconferencing platforms as a means for generating good interview material. Susie Weller (2017), for example, was able to compare rapport in interviews that she conducted via Skype and in person with the same participants over the course of her qualitative longitudinal research with young people. She found that the ordinariness and informality of mediated communication for most young people aids disclosure and can counter the 'pressure of presence', concluding that the feeling of temporal and emotional connection was key in generating a richness of interaction.

Online focus groups interviews display many of the strengths and drawbacks covered earlier but are often magnified. In-person group interviews can be often difficult logistically in arranging a place and time that suits all participants and incurring travel and room hire expenses. Some of these disadvantages can be countered by undertaking the focus groups in an online environment. Participants will still interact, but it has to be borne in mind that group members are all in different places and judging cues for transitions between turns at speaking from a gallery of images. Researchers may need to be more interventionist in this respect than they would for in-person group discussion. The most common advice about conducting video-based focus groups is to have a lower number of participants than is usual for in-person groups (ideally so that the interviewer can see all participants on their screen at once) (e.g. Lobe and Morgan 2021).

Having shifted both individual and group interviews online for her research as a result of the pandemic, Marnie Howlett (2021) raises questions about our understanding of the nature of fieldwork, when video-mediated interviewing means that geographical and private/personal boundaries become blurred. She argues that interviews can no longer be understood simply as based on personal interaction in a shared setting but also needs to be envisaged as engagement with spatio-temporal relationships and events that can occur simultaneously in digital and non-digital realms.

Conclusion

In this chapter, we have considered the importance of the setting in which qualitative interviews take place and the effects this can have on interviewer and interviewee and their interaction, influencing the type of data that can be generated. These effects can be the most general – the influence of places and spaces on identity, perceptions, memories, emotions and the interaction of hierarchies of power at different levels associated with individuals, institutions, organizations and society. And they can be very specific effects on the participants in the face-to-face interaction, including noise, interruptions and distractions. We have indicated the ideal space for the pragmatic qualitative interviewer in person and discussed types of interviews where the research activity takes place at a distance through various platforms with particular attention to video-based interviewing. In Chapter 5 we discuss the tools that can be used in qualitative interviews.

CHAPTER 5

Research Tools Used in Conducting Qualitative Interviews

Introduction

As we have stressed in this book so far, a key purpose of a qualitative interview broadly is to elicit the experiences, perceptions and feelings of the research participant/s – a sort of conversation or dialogue. It is an asymmetrical rather than an equal exchange, however. The interviewer largely delineates and controls the topic of discussion in an effort to, depending on your epistemological approach, gain access to essential meaning from, or co-generate it with, the interviewee or interviewees. Questions are the most commonly used interview tool in this endeavour, but researchers can utilize a range of other textual, visual and creative tools to engage interviewees and stimulate discussion as part of qualitative interviews, and thereby reveal aspects of participants' sense-making processes. Some argue that interviewees respond in a different way to these sorts of tools – that they access parts of personhood that interviews using words alone cannot reach.

Indeed, in addition to the relatively straightforward process of asking questions, there has been a proliferation of tools that researchers have developed to stimulate and facilitate interaction, enhance or contribute to communication and draw out (as desired) stories, accounts or responses. An interviewer can use many different techniques and tools as appropriate to the particular topic and questions of their research, the setting in which they are carrying out the interview as well as the form of the interview, and the characteristics of interviewees taking part in their research. In this chapter we begin by addressing the basic currency of qualitative interviews – talking – before moving on to address the sorts of techniques that researchers can use to augment and extend the process of asking questions: writing, seeing and creating. Under each of these broad headings, we provide illustrations of work using these tools, albeit we can only discuss a few of the available techniques to illustrate their potential.

Talking

A basic tool for researchers in asking questions in qualitative interviews is an interview or topic guide. This guide is a list of questions or subjects that need to be covered during the interview, sometimes in a particular order and way (semi-structured), sometimes not (in-depth). The interviewer follows the guide but as part of the exchange of talk during the interview is able to pursue topical trajectories that may stray from the guide when she or he feels this is fruitful and appropriate. Whether conducting a semi-structured or unstructured qualitative interview, in developing their question or topic guides researchers take into consideration the focus of inquiry, what they want to learn from the person they are speaking with, how much time they have available and the kind of access they have and how much they already know about their research topic.

The process of producing interview topics and questions for the guide, however, can seem mysterious. How does it occur? Where do you start? Kirstin Luker (2008: 168–71) provides an engaging and detailed description of how she generates interview questions and a guide. Her paper-and-pen format can easily be adapted to the use of online whiteboard and visual mapping tools:

[I] take a pack of 3 by 5 index cards and write down every single question I want to know the answer to ... I write one question per card, and I try to use the kind of easygoing, accessible language that I would use during an actual interview. . . . So instead of writing 'What motivated you to get involved in this issue?' which is the real question I'm interested in, I would get at this with a number of questions, on the assumption that few of us know our own motivations, and even when we do, we rarely think of them as 'motivations' per se. So I would jot down a series of specific, concrete questions to get to this point: 'When did you decide to get involved? What was going on in your life? Why then, and not earlier or later? Why this issue and not a closely related one? . . .

Then I take this stack of index cards . . . and I arrange them. . . . I sit down near a flat surface – for me, the living room floor has always worked just fine – and I lay out these cards in different orders. If you play around with your cards long enough, you will see that they start to 'clump'. By this I mean that there will be a sort of topic outline of the areas you're interested in, and a series of questions will fall into each topic area. Then, within each topic area, I try to arrange the questions as closely as possible to an approximation of natural language . . . how would a natural conversation about your topic go? Obviously it would move from the more general to the more specific, and from the less emotionally threatening to the more emotionally threatening . . . [and at the end] you would want to 'cool down' the interview, setting the stage for a friendly departure.

Interview guides can be quite specific, covering types of questions and how they should be asked. A number of qualitative research texts provide typologies or categories of questions and their ordering, all of which can be useful in thinking about how to ask questions. James P. Spradley, in his classic text *The Ethnographic Interview* (1979), for example, identifies and describes a number of types of questions. These include descriptive-type questions such as broad, open 'grand tours' in the tone of 'tell me about your experience of . . . ', 'what was it like being . . . ' or questions where the interviewee is asked to talk through a specific concrete example of a situation and so on. Another type of question is those that fall in the structural mode, for example, 'verification' sorts of questions about when, where and in what order something happened, or 'what do you mean by . . . ' as well clarifications and so on. And contrast-type questions include the interviewer asking the interviewee to compare their experience of one issue or person with another, such as 'what's the difference between . . . ' or rank or rate a range of experiences. We discuss more targeted types of interview questions and talking techniques, such as follow-ups and probes, further in Chapter 6 when we look at the practicalities involved in qualitative interviews.

In contrast to a detailed sequence of carefully thought-through questions, topic guides can be quite sketchy, more by way of a reminder of subjects to cover in the interview. The interviewer relies on the flow of interaction with the interviewee to steer the interview process, constructing questions about the issues to be covered as the interview progresses, rather than asking any predetermined specific types of questions. In Figure 5.1, we have reproduced an interview guide from the qualitative element of a project that set out to understand young people's experiences with workplace sexual harassment (McLaughlin et al. 2012) to show you what a topic guide of this sort might look like.

The key issue in thinking about talking techniques in interviews, though, is to come back to the fundamental issue of what the research is about. Certain types of questions will be better suited to promote interview interaction and discussion that provides answers relevant to the overarching subject of investigation, stimulating knowledge about the particular research issues as well as in keeping with the epistemological approach adopted (see Chapter 2). For example, descriptive 'grand tour' questions are an excellent fit with narrative research that seeks to elicit stories from interviewees and understand these within a broadly interpretive approach. The same issue of 'fit for purpose and approach' is true of the various types of research techniques and tools to augment and enhance interviews that we now discuss.

Writing

Written texts to stimulate talk in qualitative interviews can be produced by either the researcher or the interviewee before the interview for use during it.

A good example of researcher-generated writing to extend and enhance talk during an interview is vignettes. These are short stories or comic strips with a purpose, about characters frequently facing fictitious but realistic circumstances or dilemmas that are relevant

Workplace Harassment Interview Guide

1 Work history—before and since high school

   a. Jobs held
   b. Gender (coworkers and managers)
   c. Interactions/environment
   d. Interactions outside of work

2. Problems in the workplace

   a. Describe problems experienced
   b. Any problems you define as sexual harassment
   c. Define sexual harassment
   d. Examples of behaviors that qualify
   e. Describe harassment training

3. Feelings today

   a. How do you feel about past experiences?
   b. If happened again, how would you respond?

4. Sexual harassment in general

   a. Why does it occur?
   b. Why some are targeted and others are not?
   c. Why some tell and others do not?

5. Other forms of harassment/discrimination

   a. Housing, education, other work problems
   b. Additional information about workplace interactions

FIGURE 5.1 *Example of a topic guide (Blackstone 2019). From* Social Research: Qualitative and Quantitative Methods, *v2.0, by Amy Blackstone. Copyright © 2019 by Boston Academic Publishing, Inc. d.b.a. FlatWorld. Reprinted with permission from FlatWorld.*

to the research enquiry, but sometimes drawn from 'real life' (Sampson and Johannessen 2019). Interviewers ask interviewees to read them or read them to interviewees at a particular point in the interview and then ask them to comment on the situation. They are especially useful in research concerned with people's attitudes, beliefs and values. Vignettes are said to be especially useful in aiding interview discussion where topics are sensitive and interviewees may feel awkward talking about particular issues. For example, Wendy Aujla (2020) used a vignette in interviews with police officers regarding 'honor'-based crimes and forced marriages within the context of domestic violence. She argues that the vignette allowed for a rich in-depth discussion without participants feeling pressured in talking about a difficult topic. We reproduce the vignette from this research as an illustration in Figure 5.2.

Figure 5.2 is a relatively simple vignette. Other researchers have developed the potential of the vignette technique further. They create a series of linked stories termed 'soap opera style' or

Nina, age 17, is seen by a close family friend kissing her boyfriend on a movie date. Usually she is careful to tell lies, such as "I am going to work," to hide the relationship. Her father often asks the brother to follow her places, and he constantly checks on her whereabouts.

When the family friend reports the kiss, Nina's father confronts her for the behaviour and then blames Nina's mother for failing to keep an eye on her own daughter. The father starts yelling about his daughter wearing makeup and running around with boys, and claims that this Western lifestyle brings shame. Nina's brother agrees with their father and threatens to kill the boyfriend. The father slaps Nina across the face, saying, "What kind of daughter are you; how will I face the community? You have disrespected me and disgraced this family. I wish you were dead."

Out of fear Nina escapes to a friend's place where she is encouraged by the friend's parents to report the incident to the police instead of eloping with her boyfriend. When the police arrive at her family's home, the brother says there should be no concerns as the family is discussing preparations for his sister's wedding. The mother calls Nina's cell phone and begs her to come home to avoid further community accusations. The mother tells her to end the current relationship because her father is planning her marriage to another man from a conservative family. Under pressure, Nina agrees to the forced marriage, and tries to defend herself by saying everything is based on rumours.

1. Describe your initial thoughts about what is happening in the scenario.
2. What parts of the vignette stood out to you, and why?
3. How would the police respond to the scenario, and what influences their response?
4. How comfortable would law enforcers (police officers) feel in investigating and reporting similar situations?
5. What experiences or situations have you heard of that are similar to the one presented in the scenario? If so, tell me more about them.
6. What else concerns you about this scenario? Any other comments?

FIGURE 5.2 *Example of a vignette used in Aujla (2020). Reproduced under CC BY-NC-4.0 licence.*

'developmental' vignettes that can be used in in-depth interview research (Finch 1987; Jenkins et al. 2010). Discussion of the characters, dilemmas faced and options available to them in one vignette leads to another vignette in which the characters have moved on in their situation and thus face further dilemmas and options. Three or four complex vignettes probably are the limit; otherwise, the thread of stories and details can be difficult for interviewees to follow.

Written texts generated by an interviewee can be unsolicited or solicited. They can stand alone as research data, but here we are concerned with their use as an aid in interviews. Where materials are unsolicited, they already exist prior to the research, say in the form of daily blog that can be followed up and discussed in an interview with the blogger. Solicited writing is produced specifically for the research. Researchers ask participants if they would undertake to produce the documents prior to the interview and give them instructions about how to do this. The texts are then used as the basis for discussion during a later face-to-face interview. Here we consider solicited diary material as illustration of the potential of this technique. Solicited diaries may be audio or video or written, and we focus on a written diary example in this section.

Sarah Linn used solicited diaries coupled with individual and focus group interviews as a means of exploring the lived experiences of refugee women in urban areas of Amman and Beirut (2021). Linn envisaged the diaries as extending the women's interview voices, giving them time and space to reflect on their emotional experiences of home in exile and complementing the interview focus on the everyday experiences of their host cities. For Linn, then, solicited diaries can fit with a transformative emancipatory approach. There were, however, issues when it came to literacy given that Linn's diary method took a written form. Further, Linn's intention was to give participants a notebook with instructions about how to complete the diaries over a four-week period, with a focus on emotional reflection. In one setting though the women began keeping their diaries before the briefing and thus elaborated on the issues they discussed in interviews and did not date their entries. This illustrates the importance of the instructions provided to research participants for the way that they keep their diaries.

Seeing

As well as text, researchers can use images in interviews to facilitate talk – often referred to as elicitation. In this section, we look at two elicitation techniques in particular: photos and graphics. Some argue that such visual images evoke deeper elements of human consciousness than do words and provide interviewers with a different order of participant responses, drawing out tacit knowledge, and latent memories and emotions (Harper 2012), which makes it attractive for researchers taking a psychoanalytic philosophical approach (see Chapter 2). There are also arguments that these visual elicitation techniques privilege the authority of the interviewee rather than the interviewer, fitting with an emancipatory approach (Harper 2012).

Photo-elicitation

Photo-elicitation is often thought of as a novel research tool but in fact has a history stretching back to the mid-twentieth century as a technique used in anthropological studies. The use of photographs, or indeed other visual images (such as paintings, graffiti, advertisements and movie clips), as a stimulus during qualitative interviews can draw on materials that are in existence prior to the research process and are brought to the interview either by interviewer or by interviewee, or they can be generated specifically as part of the research process by the interviewee solely or in collaboration with the researcher (and may be referred to as photovoice). The photos may be general, collective or specific to the interviewee, and may be institutional (class of 1989), of an era (civil rights movement in the 1960s) or intimate (family birthday party).

For example, in a form of participatory research, Keri Rodriguez and colleagues (2019) provided homeless and marginally housed veterans with a digital camera and memory card to take photographs of their experience with health and wellness. They then explored what these images meant to the veterans literally and metaphorically through discussion in interviews, drawing out dimensions of the veterans' complex and holistic understandings of health and wellness that Rodriguez and colleagues argue would not otherwise be apparent. Also in collaborative mode, but using interviewee's own pre-existing pictures, Rebecca Mott and colleagues (2021) asked young people living on farms to locate photographs they felt depicted what it meant to be a livestock producer throughout childhood and then interviewed them about the images and their memories. In contrast, Karen Henwood and colleagues (2011) used researcher-selected photo images of fatherhood from different eras (Victorian through to contemporary) in their longitudinal psychosocial study of men's accounts of first-time fatherhood. They asked their interviewees to comment upon these photos in interviews in an effort to understand the way in which the men formulated and made sense of their aspirations for modern fatherhood within and against dominant socio-historical representations of fathers.

The photovoice method, as part of a transformative agenda led by research participants, has also been re-envisioned by Indigenous researchers. Beaudin Bennett and colleagues (2019) discuss participant-directed Indigenization of photovoice, adapting the method to the world views of Indigenous communities. In their case, this involved participants identifying and presenting not just photos but also paintings and other images, and ensuring discussion following the protocols of a communal learning circle. In the circle format, any participant could talk about the meaning of an image they had brought along or talk about the meaning of an image another participant had shared, or pass. This Gaataa'aabing visual method was co-created with Anishinaabek people in Ontario, Canada, but the researchers believe that the method's focus on the integration of the cultural values of the Indigenous community and focus on concrete community outcomes will resonate with Indigenous groups more widely.

Graphic Elicitation

Graphic elicitation techniques cover a wide range of interview tools produced as part of qualitative interviews, to capture and represent relationships, feelings and so on. Timelines, for example, consist of a drawn line, straight or winding, representing time passing, along which interviewees mark significant events and aspects of personal experience over the course of their life as a whole or specific parts of it. Annie Chen (2018) describes the use of interviewee-generated timelines, to elicit interviewees' recollections and reflections on their experience of chronic illness. They argue that the timeline drawing activity gave participants the opportunity to share their illness journeys from their own perspective and aided reflection during the interview.

Graphic tools can also attempt to represent affect, using actual or metaphorical maps. Maps of a geographical area or location can be used in qualitative interviews to capture and talk about the emotions associated with different places and spaces. For example, researchers have used participatory mapping and qualitative geographical information system (GIS) methods in interviewing children about their perceptions of their school journey experiences (Wilson et al. 2019) and have asked staff living in a community of adults with learning disabilities to locate emotions they experienced in the community house using different coloured stickers on a floor plan (McGrath et al. 2019).

Metaphorically, as part of her groundbreaking anthropological study of households as resource systems, Sandra Wallman (1984) developed two linked network maps to use with interviewees. Each map consisted of concentric rings around the household unit with different segments or slices of the pie for kin, non-kin and difficult relationships, respectively. Both maps recorded closeness of different kinds: one allowed the interviewee to record significant others in terms of geographical distance; the other recorded the same people in terms of their emotional closeness in the interviewee's view. Similar concentric circle or linked circle methods to capture relationships and their significance include what have been referred to as social convey diagrams, ecomaps, genograms and sociograms. Andreas Herz and Alice Altissimo (2021) undertook a qualitative study of the significance of social networks for transnational youth mobility. They used large sheets of paper with concentric circle network maps during interviews, asking interviewees to use Post-it notes to represent significant people and organizations and to draw and describe connections between them. We reproduce an example from their study in Figure 5.3.

Most of these tools have been used with individual interviewees, but a graphic elicitation technique designed explicitly to capture interaction between research participants is the household portrait method developed by Andrea Doucet (2001). Emily Christopher (2021) used this tool to study gendered divisions and implicit

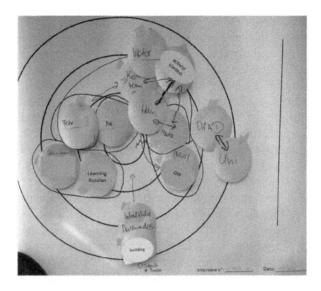

FIGURE 5.3 *Tim's sociogram (Herz and Altissimo 2021: 506).*
Reproduced under CC BY-NC-4.0 licence.

understandings of household labour among working parent, heterosexual couples. The couple is asked to work together to place stickers with colour-coded household tasks and responsibilities onto a grid indicating whether and to what extent the activity was undertaken by the man or woman. The interviewer is present during this activity and can ask for, or be subject to, clarification or explanation as it happens. The graphic 'portrait' that results from the collaborative sorting of household tasks and responsibilities forms data in itself, but the couple's discussion together and with the researcher during the co-production is further richer data.

Creating

All the interview tools discussed so far – talking, writing and seeing – are creative, but some tools can involve research participants in more extended and extensive projects that can be talked about in qualitative interviews in order to explore perceptions, emotions, memories, identities and so on. Here we provide some interesting examples to show the potential of creating techniques.

Building on a materialist notion of research as assemblage, Carrie Safron (2020) adopted magazine scrapbooking as part of a visual ethnography of an urban after-school programme. Scrapbooks usually involve collages of cuttings, drawings and writing. Working with health and fitness-related magazines, Safron worked with Black and Latinx youth on the programme to rip or cut parts of text and images from the magazines into scrapbooks. In group discussions and follow-up individual interviews, the researcher and young people reflected on the scrapbooks that they had produced and what they said about commercial ideas of a fit and healthy body. Another embodiment-focused project used the body-mapping method (Klein and Milner 2019), guided by a transformative emancipatory approach. The method involves the researcher and interviewee co-creating a life-size outline of the participant's body on paper. In discussion during the interview, the participant decorates the body map. This is followed by the interviewee producing a short testimony explaining their body map.

Creating methods are often located within an emancipatory approach to research. Identity boxes were conceived by Nicole Brown (2019) as facilitating a co-productive piece of research on sensory and bodily experiences of chronic illness. Participants were provided with questions, such as 'what affects you?' and 'how do others see you?', and asked to find objects that would represent their answer. They then placed objects into their identity box and emailed a photo of their box along with a brief explanation of the objects and what they represented to the researcher. The aim of the identity box was to provide participants with a way of focusing and deepening reflections on their experiences. The box activity was followed by a video-conference interview where participants elaborated on the objects and their meaning.

The idea of 'metaphorical models' or 'Make-Think-Talk' method, where interviewees are asked to make visual objects (video, collage, drawing, moulding etc.) and then interpret them in interviews, has been propounded by David Gauntlett (e.g. Culpepper and Gauntlett 2021). People may, for example, be asked to create a model of how they feel on a Friday afternoon or to build a model that overviews the different aspects of their identity or their vision for reorganization of their workplace. The research data are not only the creative product but also the discussion of the production process and choices made and crucially the interviewees' interpretation of what they have produced. The method can be used with individuals or groups of people. The plastic building brick format LEGO® has been used in research into conceptions of international education among a diverse group of professionals, for example, with the play element argued to allow equality of voice among participants to express their vision and to listen and connect to that of others (McCusker 2020).

Conclusion

The research techniques for use in and with qualitative interviews that we have discussed in this chapter are not exhaustive. What we have done though, we hope, is to open the qualitative interviewer's mind to, and whet their appetite for, the possibilities and potential of a range of writing, seeing and creating tools to aid, stimulate, facilitate, enhance, draw out, augment, extend and contribute to talking. As well as not being exhaustive, the tools to use alongside talking are not exclusive. We have discussed writing, seeing and creating under separate headings, illustrated by their distinct use in particular studies, but they can be used in various combinations in a single project, depending on the research aims and the data needed to meet them. Whatever the techniques and tools used in qualitative interviews, however, careful questioning, listening and responding remain important – part of our concern in the next chapter.

CHAPTER 6

The Practicalities Involved in Conducting Qualitative Interviews

Introduction

In this chapter, we look at some of the practical issues involved in preparation for and during qualitative interviews. In other words, we address the practicalities of qualitative interviewing practice – the routine and taken-for-granted processes and activities that are part of the generation of interviews: what interviewers 'do'.

We cover preparation for interviews in terms of how many interviews need to be conducted, gaining informed consent for participation in interviews and equipment for recording interviews. And we deal with the mundane but crucial social interaction of conducting interviews: how to start an interview, how to listen and ask questions during an interview and how to finish an interview.

How Many Interviews?

Both students and more experienced researchers can be preoccupied with the question of how many interviews they should do when they are conducting a piece of qualitative empirical work. The topic frequently forms a thread on online discussion forums such as 'Methodspace' and 'Postgraduate Forum'.

The concept of saturation is often mooted as the ideal guide for the number of interviews to be conducted, especially where researchers are taking an interpretive, grounded approach. That is, qualitative interviewers should continue sampling and identifying cases until their interviewees are not telling them anything that they have not heard before. Thus, rather than the number in a sample being representative of types of people as in quantitative research, in qualitative research, it is the range of meanings that should determine the numbers of interviewees in a study. Using data saturation is challenging for many qualitative interviewers, however, because sampling, data collection and data analysis have to be combined, and it is not possible to specify how many interviews are necessary in advance. This can be a problem where project proposals may require researchers to state a number. But further, the notion of data saturation is often philosophically in tension with interpretive approaches where qualitative researchers regard meaning as generated rather than excavated in data analysis (Braun and Clarke 2021).

A collection and review of advice from noted qualitative interview methodologists on the question of 'how many qualitative interviews is enough?' finds the recurring answer, 'it depends' (Baker and Edwards 2012). The guidance offered by contributors as to what the number of interviews depends upon includes the following:

- *Epistemological and methodological questions* about the nature and purpose of the research: whether the focus of the objectives and of analysis is on commonality or difference or uniqueness or complexity or comparison or instances. A single case is sufficient if it is unique and not comparable or to establish if something is possible, for example, but greater numbers are required to compare particular groups. A key issue is the ability to build a convincing narrative based on rich detail and complexity.

- *Practical issues* such as the level of degree, the time and finances available and institutional committee requirements. How much time is available to find and keep in contact with participants and complete the project, for example? And will research ethics committees or upgrade boards have a view on appropriate numbers?

- Linked to the last point and cutting across epistemology and practicality, the judgement of the *epistemic community* in which a student or researcher wishes to be or is located is an issue. What size of sample or number of cases will satisfy mentors, peers and readers, and forestall critics? For example, one interview is considered valid evidence in oral history.

Some contributors to the collection do provide rough numbers to guide those who are desperate: 1 (Passerini and Sandino); between 12 and 60, with a mean of 30 (Adler and Adler); and 20 for masters and 50 for doctoral theses (Ragin). There have been a number of spirited exchanges about whether and how sample size may be determined (see e.g. Sim et al. 2018, for overview and argument, and Blaikie 2018 for response). This overall diversity in discussions of how many qualitative interviews are enough reveals the importance of the epistemological and methodological, practical and epistemic community issues that comprise the 'it depends' of the answer.

Information Leaflets and Consent Forms

Most institutions require staff and students to gain ethical approval for their research before they begin their studies, and most social researchers regard fully informing potential participants about the research project in which they are being asked to participate, and gaining their informed – and often written – consent, as ethical good practice (see Chapter 2 on institutional research governance). For example, the research ethics committee of one of our institutions advises that information leaflets cover what the research is about, why the person has been chosen, what taking part in the study will involve, any benefits or risks involved, promises of confidentiality and anonymity, rights to withdraw, who to approach for further information or to complain to about the research process and so on. Similarly, it is recommended that the consent form consists of a series of tick box statements about having read the information sheet, agreeing for their data to be used and stored for research purposes and their participation being voluntary, which the potential participant should then sign.

All social research is subject to debates about who can and should consent in the case of children and vulnerable adults; questions about whether consent can ever be *fully* informed where researchers themselves are not always sure what the outcomes and uses of the data may be before they start; discussion about whether consent is the one-off process implied by ethics committee processes; concerns that the bureaucratization of consent procedures may shift research participation towards those who are comfortable with bureaucracy and signing forms, and interventions that reveal the mismatch between institutional requirements and Indigenous word views (Klykken 2021, Tauri 2017, Wiles 2012). Nonetheless, gaining informed consent in qualitative research also raises method-specific ethical issues in relation to interviewing.

In the case of interviews, potential interviewees usually are briefed about the purpose and process of the interview and how long it is estimated that it will last when invited to participate. Once they have agreed to participate, they are asked again for their consent at the start of the interview. Some, however, have concerns that being too specific about the topic and questions to be addressed in the interview may shape interviewees' answers in particular ways that may not be helpful to the research endeavour (Brinkmann and Kvale 2015). Certainly if you are interested in, for example, class prejudice among the elite, it may not be a good idea to explain your research to them in those terms. Further, even if interviewees do have the research explained to them as fully as possible, consent cannot be completely informed prior to an interview given that interviews may involve greater disclosure and revelation than both interviewee and interviewer anticipated or intended.

A more fundamental challenge is to be found in arguments that the qualitative interviewing process goes beyond explaining the substantive topic of the research and the type of questions to be asked in information leaflets because the interviewer himself or herself is implicated in the process (unless an approach is adopted where the idea is to minimize the role of the interviewer as far as possible – see Chapter 2). Researchers advocating interpretivist, postmodern and/or psychoanalytic philosophical approaches to social research, such as Norman Denzin (2010), James Holstein and

Jaber Gubrium (2016), Svend Brinkmann and Steiner Kvale (2015), understand the social researcher as a fundamental, integral and significant element in the interview process, as the main instrument by which ethical decisions are made and knowledge is generated.

Tina Miller and Mary Boulton go further to argue that standardized regulation of consent procedures is increasingly ill-fitting for qualitative interviews conducted in a complex and fluid social world. Rather, they say, individual qualitative interviews need to be dealt with on their own terms, where the researchers should

> document the *process* of consent – the invitation, the response from the participant, the questions asked and answers given, the negotiation of dates and times of interviews, and so on. This is potentially a much more appropriate and useful way of working towards (and documenting) participation in research which is both informed and voluntary than asking participants to sign a consent form at the start of study. (2007: 2209, original emphasis)

In the case of qualitative longitudinal research, the fact that consent is a process is more apparent since it must be negotiated afresh for each research encounter.

Recording Equipment

In qualitative interviews, words are the main currency of the interviewing and subject to analytic interpretation; audio or video-audio recording of interview talk has become standard whether interviewing in person or via video communication platforms. Audio recording interviewees may be impossible or inappropriate in some situations, however, and sometimes interviewees may feel self-conscious about having their words recorded, or indeed the audio recorder may not work (or the interviewer cannot work it!). Interviews can still go ahead in these circumstances, with the interviewer making notes on what the interviewee says: recording talk in written note form. Indeed, some contend that recording is not necessarily the best practice for interviews, as with the slow interview technique mentioned in Chapter 2, or that not recording and taking notes is not 'second best' (Rutakumwa et al. 2020), while for others the recording device itself needs to be considered as agential in the interview process (Nordstrom 2015).

Recording qualitative interviews can be useful both during the interview itself and afterwards. During the interview, recording means that qualitative interviewers can focus on listening, probing and following up (see later) and maintaining eye contact (where culturally appropriate) with their interviewee. It can be quite distracting to have to keep making notes during the interview. But this is not to say that recording devices alleviate distractions from the talk of the interview. Interviewers can find themselves constantly checking whether or not their recording device is still working, if the microphones remain positioned closely enough to the interviewee/s to pick up their words clearly and monitoring the level of background noise (you may be able to focus on hearing the interviewee and mentally block out the music being played in the next room but the recorder will not), or worrying about stable internet connection.

As mentioned in our Chapter 2 discussion of the history of the interview in relation to technological development and the implications for producing knowledge, as technologies develop, so do the means of recording qualitative interviews – from pen and paper notes and remembered quotes written up after the interview, to bulky reel-to-reel tape recorders, to portable cassette recorders, to mini digital audio recorders, and also video recorders. Sound quality has also improved. Technology and the equipment available change rapidly, but good advice can often be found on oral history resource websites in particular, e.g. Digital Omnium: https://digitalomnium.com/.

Kirstin Luker explains that recording interviewees' words means that the metaphors or expressions and their emotional timbre and tone of voice during the interview – the way people say what they say – remains accessible long after the interview itself: 'Months and even years into a study, when I've finally figured out what the elements of my categories are, I go back to my very first interviews, and there they are, although my ear was not sophisticated enough to recognize them at the time' (2008: 174). And when it comes to writing up research, recording what an interviewee has said means that researchers can provide verbatim quotes.

This access to the talk of the interview through recording is not necessarily an unmitigated good. Some argue that the improvement of quality in interview recording devices can give a sense of being present at the interview later, a form of realist innocence (Nordstrom 2015). Les Back muses on the recording of interviews as both enabling and limiting:

> Enabling in the sense that it allowed for the voices of people to be faithfully transcribed with accuracy. Paradoxically, the fact that the recorder captured the voice and the precise detail of what informants said meant that social researchers have become less attentive as observers. The tacit belief that the researcher needed merely to attend to what was said has limited the forms of empirical documentation. (2010: 23, 24)

The key issue here, then, is for qualitative interviewers to reflect carefully on the analytic status that they bestow on recorded accounts and their own philosophical stance.

Starting an Interview

You have your interviewee, consent has been gained, the recording device is working and the qualitative interview can start. But how is it best to begin? Luker recommends what she refers to as 'the hook' to start the conversation about the topic of research. The 'hook' is how she explains the study she is conducting to the people she is about to interview – yet again:

> Yes, I know that you probably used your hook when you talked to your interviewees on the phone to get them to agree to be interviewed; you may well have told them the hook when you first wrote them a letter asking if you could interview them; and there may even be a version of your hook in a consent form. . . . But you can never tell people too often what your study is about, why you are interested in it, why *they* should be interested in it, and most important, why the person you are interviewing is *the* key person needed to help you understand this puzzling case that you are studying with such intensity. (2008: 171).

Once the stage for the interview has been set through the hook, qualitative interviewers often like to ask if the interviewee has any questions about the interview before they begin. They then open the interview 'proper' by asking general, broad questions of the 'grand tour' type mentioned in Chapter 5, for example: 'Please tell me how you started skydiving.' As the interview progresses, the questions gradually focus on more specific and targeted enquiries. Liselott Aarsand and Pål Aarsand (2019) discuss the process of starting an interview as 'getting into the interviewer and interviewee position' and achieving the 'topic talk' that is the research focus.

Active Listening, Probing and Following Up

A qualitative interview is often thought about in terms of the interviewer asking questions and the interviewee responding to them. In this respect, Luker has the idea of 'turn signals' between different aspects of the research topic that comprise the interview, which alert the interviewee that you are shifting from the issue that you have just asked them about and they are currently discussing to another area of the research topic. An example that she gives is: 'Up to now, we've been talking about your childhood. Now I'd like to ask you about [fill in the blank]' (2008: 170–1). But interviewees are not just passive respondents, and interviewers have to fit themselves around what the interviewee is telling them and respond in turn with appropriate questions that fit into the 'natural' flow of the discussion.

Indeed, overall the process of qualitative interviews requires a lot of concentration and effort on the part of the interviewer. Often referred to as 'active listening', interviewing involves the qualitative researcher in multitasking. At any one time, you may simultaneously be listening to what your interviewee or interviewees are saying at that moment and paying attention to what they are trying to convey, alongside considering whether or not what the interviewee is talking about is relevant to, or is going somewhere relevant to your research topic, while also being open to new avenues being opened up for how you think about your research topic. You may also concurrently be recalling something the interviewee said earlier in the interview, thinking about how to respond to what they are currently talking about, as well as thinking about how to put your next question that may involve a 'turn signal'. All of this while also pragmatically keeping an eye on time and monitoring your recording equipment.

Actively listening and attending to what interviewees are saying is a crucial skill for a qualitative interviewer as part of the social interaction of interviews. It involves being attuned, alert and attentive to what the interviewee is telling you or even not telling you. Listening well is a qualitative interviewing skill that often goes unremarked in favour of a focus on how to ask questions, yet it is the foundation of being able to respond to what the interviewee is saying, and able to probe and follow up their answers to your questions effectively and sensitively.

Probing and following up in interviews are 'active listening' techniques by which qualitative interviewers attempt to get an interviewee to open up, provide more information, and elaborate and expand on what they have said. It is difficult to plan probes in advance because they are responses to what an interviewee is saying at the time in the interview, but it is useful to have a sense of the range of probes that a qualitative interviewer can use. In a classic text, H. Russell Bernard (2000) delineates seven ways of probing during qualitative interviews, most of which require prudent and well-judged use at different points within a single interview:

- *Silence.* This probe involves being quiet once an interviewee appears to have finished answering a question, perhaps nodding your head, and waiting for an interviewee to continue and add more to the topic they were discussing. It provides interviewees with time to reflect. Allowing silence to endure in an interview can be very difficult for interviewers but effective if used sparingly.

- *Echo.* This is where an interviewer repeats the last point that the interviewee has said and is useful especially when they have been describing a process or event. Bernard asserts that this probe shows the interviewee that you have understood what they have said so far and encourages them to continue and expand.

- *Uh-huh.* Saying 'yes', 'I see', 'right' and so on as an interviewee talks affirms what the interviewee has said. It can act rather like silent nodding of your head.

- *Tell-me-more*. After an interviewee has answered a question, this probe encourages interviewees to expand and go further through follow on questions along the lines of, 'Why do you feel like that about it?' 'Can you tell me more about that?' 'What did you mean when you said . . .?' 'What did you do then?' and so on.

- *Long question*. These sorts of probes can help at the beginning of interviews in the grand tour mould. Bernard gives the example of when he asked sponge divers he was interviewing, 'Tell me about diving into really deep water. What do you do to get ready, and how do you ascend and descend? What's it like down there?' (2000: 198). He also says that threatening or sensitive questions (he gives the example of condom use) can benefit from a long rambling run-up to them.

- *Leading*. These are directive probes – though as Bernard points out, any question leads in an interview. The idea of asking leading questions is often treated in introductory methods textbooks for students as if it were an anathema, with concerns about 'bias'. The assumption is that if you ask a leading question, then the answer you get will be produced by the way the question is put such as, 'Do you think that this is a really bad way of behaving?' Qualitative interviewers with experience, however, know that this is rarely the case. Interviewees are perfectly capable of telling you that you do not understand what they mean; that actually they don't 'think it's a really bad way of behaving' at all.

- *Baiting*. Bernard says this sort of probe is a 'phased assertion' in which the interviewer acts as if they already know something. He contends that either people then feel comfortable opening up or are likely to correct you if they think that you have got the wrong idea.

Bernard also provides advice on dealing with interviewees who say either too much or too little during an interview. 'Verbal' interviewees are very likely to go off on a tangent as they tell you much more than you need to know for your research topic (but bearing in mind that this may take you into new insights on what is relevant to your research). Barnard recommends 'graceful' interruption and moving the interview back on track. 'Non-verbal' interviewees provide monosyllabic or 'don't know' responses to questions. As Bernard says: '[S]ometimes you can get beyond this, sometimes you can't.' If you can't, then it is best to 'cut your losses' (2000: 200). Indeed, often qualitative interviewers can feel themselves to be failures if they have to give up on an interview, but this is not the case. There is little to be gained by continuing on for the sake of it and ending an interview may sometimes be the wisest course of action.

Finishing an Interview

By the time an interview ends, qualitative interviewers will probably have spent an hour or more asking their interviewee/s questions and the interviewees will have been telling them about their lives. This can create a sort of intimate link that is broken suddenly when the interview ends. Luker (2008) discusses the 'cool down' to 'finish up and let go of the interview' that enables both interviewer and interviewee to detach themselves from each other gradually, through final questions that focus on the future or ask the interviewee to review their experience or identify the most important thing that they feel they have discussed or mentioned. It is also important finally to thank the interviewee. Luker warns, however, that it might be an idea to keep your audio recorder handy at this point because sometimes interviewees can start opening up again with fascinating information just after the recorder has been turned off. Such a practice, however, has ethical dimensions – Does the participant need to consent explicitly to the further recording of their words after they may assume that the research interview has finished?

The discussion of practicalities in this chapter may seem rather mechanistic at points (e.g. probes such as repeating the point the interviewee makes). Interviews can be situations of visceral dynamics, however, involving power and emotions – as we discuss in the next chapter.

CHAPTER 7

Power and Emotional Dynamics in Qualitative Interviews

Introduction

Issues of power and emotion in social research generally, and within the qualitative interview situation especially, have been the subject of attention in the methods literature for some time, across a range of philosophical approaches. In qualitative interviewing, researchers attempt to create an interaction that goes beyond a conversational exchange, where their interviewees feel safe enough to talk openly about their experiences and understandings. To some extent then, researchers attempt to exercise power to generate an atmosphere in which interviewees will experience emotions of rapport that are beneficial for the interview. But researchers also pay attention to the dynamics of power and emotions in interviews because they are concerned about the ethics of the research process as well as the insights into the topic under investigation that such reflection can generate – the interactional dynamics of qualitative research interviews (Roulston 2019b). These two sides of interviews have been termed 'conquest or communion', with interviewers exercising power through the application of questioning techniques such as probing in order to generate data from interviewees (see Chapter 6) but also experiencing an emotional interdependency with their interviewees.

From a psychosocial perspective in particular, power and emotions come together in both conscious and unconscious ways in a qualitative research interview. As noted in Chapter 2, at the heart of a psychoanalytic perspective on the interview is the notion of a 'defended subject'. In this view, anxiety is inherent in the human condition and consequently unconscious defences against anxieties come into play for both interviewee and interviewer and are part of the dynamics of the interview (as in all types of relations between people) (Brinkmann and Kvale 2015). But power and emotions are also present in everyday lives and interactions in a more social-structural, relational manner. Society consists of groups of people sharply divided from one another. Social divisions refer to social patterns of substantial and distinctive material and cultural differences between people – around race, social class, sexuality, religion and so on – where the social positioning of members of certain categories gives them a greater share of resources and power over the way that society is organized (Payne 2013). These hierarchies and inequalities can shape and be traced in interview interactions.

In this chapter, we consider some of the dynamics of power asymmetries and interplays of emotion discernible when interviewer and interviewee come together in the qualitative interview situation.

The Dynamics of Power in Interviews

By its nature interview research involves asymmetries of power; it is the interviewer who defines the situation and who frames the topic and course of the interview (Brinkmann and Kvale 2015). But the situation is more complex than the researcher inhabiting a more powerful and knowledgeable position than the (vulnerable) participants who they are interviewing. Although it is important to acknowledge the power of the researcher's position, there is a 'flip side' to the interview encounter where qualitative researchers may feel themselves physically and emotionally vulnerable, navigating an unfamiliar built environment, enduring unsavoury (to the researcher) interview conditions and facing unpredictable participant behaviour (Bashir 2020).

Interview interactions themselves are imbued with power relations. Tea Torbenfeldt Bengtsson and Lars Fynbo (2017) discuss the way that silence can be an illuminating power dynamic in a qualitative interview setting, not as the interview failure that it may be taken for. Drawing on their studies involving risk-takers (drugs, crime and drink-driving), they argue that the substantive research focus framed them and their interviewees in relation to each other. The researchers demonstrate how their interviewees could use silence to resist a 'social deviant' labelling, while silence from qualitative interviewers could involve both losing control of an interview and the exercise of power as a strategy to elicit interviewee talk. One example from their interview exchanges involves both the interviewee, Freddy, and the interviewer exercising the power of silence (p. 26):

Freddy: Well, first of all, drink-driving is stupid - - - [silence, 3 seconds].
Interviewer: Okay.
Freddy: I'll say that it's better to learn this early in life.
Interviewer: Yes.
Freddy: - - - [silence, 3 seconds] And - - - [silence, 3 seconds] I've learned a lot from this - - - [silence, 3 seconds] after I was arrested.
Interviewer: Yes.
Freddy: - - - [silence, 3 seconds]
Interviewer: Have you really?

An additional dimension is brought to the flows of power between interviewer and interviewee in qualitative research, when an interpreter is part of the process as a language and cultural broker in cross-cultural research. Kim Ozano provides a knotty picture of her cross-cultural, cross-language qualitative research project in rural Cambodia, working with local research assistants who also acted as interpreters (Ozano and Khatri 2018). She details the implications of the political forces and established social hierarchical power structures that cut across the non-hierarchical grounding and open lines of communication she sought to establish:

> I began with asking prepared open questions such as 'How did the plan go?' 'What worked well or didn't work so well?' 'How did it make you feel?' 'What experiences did you have when implementing the action plan?' however we received short answers such as 'it was fine', 'no problem', 'it is done, don't worry'. We struggled to get any additional details of what had transpired. . . . [The research assistants] highlighted that the open questions I was asking were not the 'Cambodian way'; and they themselves were not familiar with this method of inquiry and struggled to imagine what they would answer in a similar situation. (2018: 196)

So far we have been concerned with the way that power can shift around over the course of an interview as a result of the positioning of all participants within the interview situation itself. However, we also need to take into account the way that social divisions and hierarchies around class, gender, race, ethnicity, age and other aspects of social status articulate with this situation and further mediate power relations. Here, we consider marginality and elite group membership. A recurring theme is the extent to which interviewers are insider members or outsider non-members of the interviewee group.

Interviewing Members of Marginalized Groups

Quite a lot of interview research is carried out with social groups who are marginalized in society. The ways that social research focuses on the lives of the powerless in the interests of the powerful, with research funding channelled along these lines, has long been noted (e.g. Bell 1978; Orlans 1971), with Howard S. Becker posing his oft-quoted question: Whose side are you on? in 1967. On the one hand, there are arguments that a focus on the interview accounts of marginalized groups serves only to perpetuate their exclusion and increase perceptions of them as problematic, confirming and legitimizing the status quo of inequality (Briggs 2003). From Indigenous and First Nation perspectives, for example, the standard interview method is rooted in asymmetrical power relations, and their substantive focus is shaped by Western imperialist frameworks that position Indigenous peoples' attitudes and behaviour as deficient and as problems (Smith 2021). On the other hand, researchers can feel a commitment to making audible what they regard as the 'silenced' voices and perspectives of the marginalized, for example, those who are working from transformative approaches that seek to minimize the power differential in the research interview setting and, crucially, to further social justice and realize social change (see Chapter 2).

The implication of an interviewer's 'positionality' (social status and identity) in relation to an interviewee is a key focus of discussions, with recurring themes being how social divisions between interviewer and interviewee may shape an interview and the extent to which unspoken assumptions are a feature of interviews where interviewer and interviewee share membership of a marginalized group. In this section, we look at the nuances of situations where an interviewer may or may not share a marginalized status with their interviewee. This is by no means a comprehensive coverage of marginalized groups (e.g. Melanie Nind 2020, on inclusive research methods), but it does highlight some general issues of power in interviews.

A key debate about feminist interviewing has been around shared gender positionality: women researchers interviewing women participants. Some argue that in this situation, interviewer and interviewee are both 'inside the culture' of being women in a male-dominated society and engage with each other on that level: 'A feminist interviewing women is by definition both "inside" the culture and participating in that which she is observing' (Oakley 1981: 53). A feminist interview is presented as involving minimal power hierarchies, generating rapport and reciprocity between interviewer and interviewee. Others, however, take a more critical view, raising concerns about the way that this very connection could be to the detriment of interviewees, where intimate rapport is performed instrumentally to draw them out in order to get 'good' data and also raises an essentialized version of gender (see the review of issues by Rachel Thwaites 2017). We return later to the point about detriments inherent in pursuing rapport in the section discussing emotions in the interview process.

Of course, researchers and participants in qualitative interview studies will not always be 'gender matched'. A number of researcher accounts consider uneven power tensions when the interviewer holds a gendered outsider position in relation to their interviewees, with most addressing women interviewing men and less attention to men as researchers. Issues raised in these cross-gender interview discussions include cautious rapport, risk and safety, and gendered behavioural norms and identities (Galam 2015; Lefkowich 2019). Queer scholars can have their embodiment and identity erased, challenged and disrespected by participants in qualitative interview studies, depending on the research context, notably where they are differences between them and their research participants but also where there are similarities. Baker Rogers (2021), for example, describes an unstable insider positioning during their research interviews with trans men in the southeastern United States, where to their surprise they faced misgendering by interviewees.

Yet other social divisions intersect and articulate with gender. For example, there can be divisions between women as interviewers and research participants on the basis of age, with interview power dynamics playing out around generational life experiences (Jen et al. 2020). Race and ethnicity in particular has been the subject of attention in the interview situation, with debates about whether or not interviewers who are researching people from minority ethnic backgrounds need to share 'race' with their interviewees in order to generate 'better' or more 'authentic' data. One study of mono-racial and inter-racial qualitative interview situations conducted in the United States, however, found that while shared race often meant shared understandings, in the case of racial divisions, acknowledging difference seemed important to establishing rapport (Mizock et al. 2011). The raced dynamics of interviewing can be more complex, however. Joanne Britton (2020) considers the multi-layered sets of power relations around whiteness in her interviews with Pakistani Muslim men in the north of England, as a form of insider (partner of a Pakistani Muslim man) as well as outsider (white female researcher):

Whiteness played an integral part in interviews, including when I distanced myself from it in order to establish rapport and facilitate disclosure . . . overstating my closeness to Pakistani culture. In doing so, I colluded in a common sense, essentialist understanding of culture and ethnicity in order to stress commonalities. (p. 344–5)

Yet at the same time, 'Participants were arguably willing to disclose sensitive details about their personal lives because they positioned me as an outsider, specifically a white woman with less conservative social values' (p. 346). Such gendered performative distancing and closeness echoes the debate in feminist interviewing about the instrumental exploitation of rapport.

Even where interviewee and interviewer share membership of a marginalized minority group, social divisions and power are not eradicated. Maisha Islam reflects on the tensions that arose where she conducted qualitative interviews with Muslim students about their sense of belonging in UK higher education. While she asserted an instrumental insider position in accessing potential research interviewees ('help a sister'), during the interviews themselves identity power dynamics could shift. More conservative Islamic participants could challenge her 'Muslimness', which Islam found an uncomfortable experience:

This experience made me contemplate the purpose of undertaking this research, especially if it meant having harassing and uncomfortable encounters. Additionally, I questioned whether my other identities (i.e. holding a liberal outlook) were at odds with my Muslim identity, and to what extent it gave me 'insider authority' to speak of Muslim experiences. (2020: 512)

Minelle Mahtani also challenges any simplistic notions of shared identities between interviewers and interviewees on the basis of race in a critical reflection on her own research process in a study of mixed-race women. While she and interviewees shared rapport and expectations of mutual recognition around mixedness, she shows how these are cross-cut with various social cleavages that separated them. Mahtani also reveals the potential drawbacks of similarity for the interview as a data-generating process:

During the research process, there were certainly times when my own status as a mixed-race woman of Indian and Iranian descent did foster dialogue. . . . During a pivotal point in our interview, one participant explained to me how she felt comfortable talking to me as a woman of mixed race. . . . However, at the same time, I was well aware that my own identification as a woman of mixed race played other roles in the interview process. For example, peppered through many interviews emerged the phrase, 'you know what I mean, Minelle' followed by a knowing glance or smile. This sort of shared complicity may have created a more comfortable space for these women to tell their stories – but also prevented them from divulging further detail. (2012: 158–9)

The social class positioning of researchers is another focus of interviewing across difference. Jina Mao and Elana Feldman (2019), for example, address interview dynamics from their position of middle-class researchers in the US context, musing on the ways that interviewers may unwittingly accentuate class boundaries and distance through assumptions, body language, speech and dress. There are, however, debates about whether or not researchers from working-class backgrounds, as a consequence of education and career, are detached from the day-to-day context that frames working-class lives. Either way, as has been pointed out, shared class position (current or ex) does not necessarily equate with similar life experiences and strong rapport (Mellor et al. 2014).

One situation where researchers will once have shared a social positioning with their interviewees but clearly no longer do so is with children. Those undertaking interview-based research with what they consider to be a marginalized social group are often motivated by a desire to counter wider societal silencing of their voices. A key point of attention is strategies for equalizing power relations between adult interviewer and child or young person interviewee, with researchers often recommending child-centred and creative research tools during interviews (e.g. Ponizovsky-Bergelson et al. 2019). There are debates about whether or not it is possible for researchers interviewing children to adopt what has been termed a 'least adult role', motivated by a desire to foreground children's voices and diffuse adult power. However, the assumption that the researcher holds power ignores the complexities of children's and young people's parallel agency and tactical use of power in an interview (Atkinson 2019; Lohmeyer 2019).

Interviewing Members of Elite Groups

In contrast to the situation where a researcher has more power than the people they are interviewing, at least in the context of wider society, it is the other way around in what is sometimes referred to as 'studying up'. Just as researchers can feel a commitment to 'giving voice' to powerless groups, they can also regard it as important to demystify the worlds of people in positions of power and privilege in society.

Those with experience of interviewing elites often emphasize the need for interviewers to have 'done their homework' before the interview and be well-prepared for it, in terms of familiarizing themselves with interviewees' background and career, or the company or institution that they represent, and/or their CVs, published views and so on, as well as ensuring that they have an in-depth grasp of the key issues concerning the topic under discussion (e.g. Lancaster 2017; Ruan 2020). Dang Vu Hoai Nam (2021) and colleagues hired luxury cars and watches in order to interview the super-rich for their study. Such strategies are regarded as a means for the researcher to attempt to decrease the status imbalance between themselves and their interviewee and to position themselves as someone who can be considered equal in terms of situated knowledge.

Several writers mention that interviewers will find themselves subject to subtle probing about their agenda and intentions for use of the interview data or even direct challenges as Nian Ruan experienced in some of her interviews with elite women academics:

> Throughout the interview, she questioned my interview protocol and study design very candidly. She disagreed with the idea that there was any gender discrimination in the careers of women scientists and thought that my study was biased from the beginning. Her very short answers to my open questions at the beginning of the interview reduced my confidence. (2020: 120)

Interviews with elite groups are often posed as a power game in which both interviewer and interviewee jockey for the upper hand. The interviewee and/or their organization is seeking to set the agenda, while the interviewer attempts control through asking their questions. Both Jana Declercq and Ricardo Ayala (2017), and Kari Lancaster (2017), respectively, interviewing Australian policymakers and global industry executives, assert that while most of the people they interviewed were enthusiastic about participating in their research, they became aware of gate-keeping and decision-making behind the scenes, exerting control over who they spoke to, and then what was discussed in the interviews: 'in relation to the elite setting, even when they have an elite position, they are not always powerful, elite individuals. In the case of [one interviewee], he is still constrained by the executive management, the parental company and company traditions concerning external communication' (Declercq and Ayala 2017: 10). As well as such informal rules of political, administrative or corporate reputation and loyalty and an 'official line' to be put forward, elite interviewees may also be subject to formal constraints on disclosure such as the UK Official Secrets Act or US Security of Information Act.

Nonetheless, Declercq and Ayala, and Lancaster, each draw attention to the professional vulnerabilities and personal uncertainties of elite interviewees and pose power dynamics in interviews with them as fluid and context dependent. For example, Lancaster reflects:

> Although my position as a Ph.D. student ordinarily may be regarded as being less powerful than that of a participant occupying a senior policy position, being from a well-known research centre and supervised by two highly respected and accomplished professors in the field (both of whom are recognised for their expertise in drug policy spheres in Australia and internationally) meant that participants were aware that their knowledge and accounts could potentially be scrutinised by senior researchers. In some interviews, this possibly generated particular 'performances' from participants who wished to appear knowledgeable in front of a critical audience. Such dynamics confuse the notion of 'studying up'. (p.97)

Several researchers who discuss conducting research interviews with members of social, economic or politically powerful groups mention variously being comfortable with or excited by their high-status participants, feeling grateful to them or steam-rollered by them, feeling privileged or patronized and/or impressed or uncomfortable about betraying their own beliefs and position. This raises the issue of emotions in the dynamics of interviews.

The Dynamics of Emotions in Interviews

By virtue of being human, researchers are not neutral and objective enquirers in qualitative interviews but are emotionally engaged participants who are sharing an experience with the interviewee. Indeed, those taking feminist and interpretive approaches to scholarship have questioned the binary opposition between reason and emotion in much Western thought, and argued that emotion is necessary to knowledge – people make sense of the social world through emotions as well as cognition or intellect (e.g. Ahmed 2017; Jaggar 1989). Acknowledgement of and reflection on the importance of emotion dynamics for both the interviewee and the interviewer as part of the construction and analysis of data can be important for the generation of knowledge (e.g. Holtan et al. 2014).

The open-ended qualitative interview, with its possibilities for discussing unexpected topics, means that emotional dynamics can be significant for the interview process. The presence of emotions in interviews is evident in our discussion of power earlier. We noted the vulnerabilities of interviewees through interviewers' generation of emotional rapport and the discomfort and risks to researcher identity in challenges to their positioning as a putative insider. The issue of participant vulnerability and emotions has received careful consideration from an ethical and moral perspective. Interviews may involve disclosure of difficult experiences that cause interviewees emotional pain to recall, and Institutional Review Boards and Ethics Committees often require researchers to have plans in place to manage the possibility of harm. In response, some have developed Distress Protocols as guides to how to respond to participant emotional discomfort in interviews (e.g. Draucker et al. 2009), and Denise Buchanan and Ian Warwick (2021: 1092) put forward the idea of 'ethical triage':

> to ascertain which actions should take priority over others. Actions taken should: prioritise the well-being of the participant, both in terms of preventing immediate and longer term harm;

adhere to the stipulations made when the ethics application was approved; be aligned with the aims of the research and serve the purpose of the research itself; and involve choosing the action that can 'bring about the greatest good'.

Recommended researcher strategies to deal with distress include stopping the interview and reviewing the participant's mental status with them, shifting the line of enquiry onto another topic, ending the interview if a period of time out is not appropriate and offering contact details of support services.

Interviews are dynamically interactive, however. There is also the issue of researchers' own emotions – for both insider and outsider research positionings, whether partial or total, and the emotional labour that researchers are engaged in as they attempt to manage their feelings and expressions during the interview interaction. There is some discussion of the emotion work that is required in the case of researching elites, including attentiveness to emotional signals as the interviewer monitors their position and actions when researching 'up' and coping with the emotive dissonance between their researcher persona and sense of 'authentic' self (Bergman Blix and Wettergren 2015). Researchers may also experience anger towards and dislike of their interviewees. Emily Graham (2022) recounts how she detested one of the interviewees in her ethnographic study, such that she had to wash herself and her clothes after her first interview with him:

> The fiction that ethnographers are objective data collecting instruments underplays the significance of researcher-researched relationships, and the way we tell our stories is less authentic if our voice is overly censored by keeping parts of our experiences off-limits. Being open to the wisdom of emotions means being open to *all* of them, not just selecting the ones which we frame as positive emotions. (para 31)

Graham concludes that distance and reflection, engaging with the emotions that she experienced as data, allowed her to reach deeper insights about her topic of study.

For the most part, researchers have discussed how interviewing on sensitive and traumatic subjects, such as death, illness, sexuality and so on, with physically and emotionally vulnerable populations can affect them. In a *Qualitative Psychology* journal special section on emotions in qualitative research (Granek 2017), contributors studying emotion-laden issues address the ways that their research affected them. Lori Ross (2017), for example, reflects on the emotional implications of her 'total insider' positionality in her longitudinal study of mental health during the transition to parenthood among sexual minority women, meaning that over time she experienced difficulties in managing an appropriately boundaried relationship and self-disclosure:

> One particularly striking example of the emotional impact of our commonalities on my capacity for empathy happened during our second interview. I was breastfeeding my baby while Nicole shared her experience of having to rush her own newborn baby to hospital with potentially serious medical complications. Despite the fact that the baby was now healthy and in her own mother's arms, this experience elicited a depth of emotion that I would consider beyond what has been termed 'feeling their stories' . . . in that I could feel the weight of Nicole's experience not only metaphorically, but literally, with respect to the infant in my own arms. My depth of feeling was explicit (reflected in the transcription as me making a 'shocked noise' and commenting to Nicole that I was holding back tears). (p.329)

In the same special section, Sara McClelland (2017) reflects on the challenges of 'vulnerable listening' drawing on her interviews with women diagnosed with Stage IV breast cancer. She points to (i) the emotional dangers of vicarious trauma and haunting sadness associated with listening to difficult accounts; (ii) the largely unacknowledged role of the listening researcher's body, in her case where she had breasts and her interviewees had theirs removed; and (iii) the experience of extreme emotions such as outrage at the material she was listening to but also at herself for being surprised about gendered injustice. Nonetheless, McClelland regards vulnerable listening as important: 'Vulnerable listening requires that the researcher understand what is happening inside of them when asking participants to speak; it highlights the difficulties as well as the generative possibilities of a listening practice' (pp. 347–8). She and other researchers discussing the strains and implications of the emotion work involved for qualitative interviewers offer recommendations for coping with them (e.g. Rogers-Shaw et al. 2021). These include regular reflexivity and recognition of the issues raised for them, the importance of self-care strategies and the significance of having good collegial support networks in place.

Again and again, researchers writing about the power and emotions in qualitative interview research argue that attending to their existence and dynamics can only enhance the knowledge generation process. Such reflection will enhance researchers' understanding of the data and their insights into the nuances of the research topic.

Conclusion

In this chapter, we have considered some of the asymmetries of power and generation of emotions in interviews. We considered how the crosscutting social positions of both interviewer and interviewee can shape and shift power dynamics during the interview in complex ways, and the gamut of emotions and emotion work that interviewing can generate and involve for both parties. Along the way, we have noted how reflecting on the dynamics of power and emotions in the interview process can provide insight into the substantive research topic. In the next chapter, we step back to the part that qualitative interviews play in the knowledge generation endeavour more broadly. We consider the strength of this method and the implications of changes in the wider environment in which qualitative interviewing is practised.

CHAPTER 8

The Changing Environment for Qualitative Interviewing

Introduction

Throughout this book, we have emphasized that it is important for the researcher to have an awareness of the philosophical and epistemological positions that underlie the qualitative interview and qualitative research in general. Further, it is the quality of analysis and the cogency of the theoretical reasoning and inferences that comprise qualitative research that is, for example, crucial to any assessment of generalization from interview findings to other contexts. In Chapter 2, we briefly considered the history of the qualitative interview and evaluated assertions that qualitative interviews and research have passed through eight or nine 'moments' since 1900 (Denzin and Lincoln 2017). We saw that there are overlapping and intersecting approaches in the moments of this model and there is no linear progression; we can say then that all of the underpinning philosophical positions upon which qualitative interviews are based that we then described in that chapter are currently in play. We did suggest a progression in the terms used to describe the person interviewed, which was seen to reflect the changing relationship between researcher and researched, interviewer and interviewee and a growing reflexivity from the researcher, under the influence of some of the philosophies outlined, particularly interpretive, transformative feminist and postmodern approaches (Chapter 1). Indeed, for many albeit not all qualitative researchers, reflexivity has become a key indicator of robustness and rigour in qualitative research, with the qualitative interviewer seeking to make the research process as transparent as possible, systematically accounting for the potential and actual effects of all of the factors involved. Qualitative interviews are social interactions with many elements coming into play. As we saw in Chapters 4 and 7 in particular, these elements include location and context, the physical and social space within which the interview takes place, power relations at the social and individual levels and a wide range of characteristics, predispositions, understandings and emotions of interviewer and interviewee. Overall then, the broader social research environment in which qualitative interviewing is practised is not static.

This book is based on an understanding of the value and importance of qualitative interviews and their contribution to a social scientific understanding of social events and interactions in context in the social world. But there are challenges for this position. In this concluding chapter, we will discuss the strengths of qualitative interviews and the implications of the wider shifting environment, digital and philosophical, in which the qualitative interview method is located.

Strengths

Qualitative interviewing is an enduring research method, chosen and used by social researchers for their research projects across the decades. The continuing popularity of qualitative interviews is rooted in the strengths of this method of investigation. People's everyday lives are conversational as they talk and interact together, and the qualitative interview is a key method of inquiry for grasping and understanding this:

> If you want to know how people understand their world and their lives, why not talk to them? Conversation is a basic mode of human interaction. Human beings talk with each other, they interact, pose questions and answer questions. Through

conversations we get to know other people, get to learn about their experiences, feelings and hopes and the world they live in. In an interview conversation, the researcher asks about, and listens to, what people themselves say about their lived world, about their dreams, fears and hopes; hears their views and opinions in their own words. (Brinkmann and Kvale 2018: 1)

Qualitative interviews facilitate the generation of material that provides rich insight into the meanings and significance that individuals and groups generate and attach to experiences, social processes, practices and events. Interviews enable researchers to understand people's lived worlds from their point of view. Through qualitative interviewing, social researchers can explore the smoothness, roughness and feeling of everyday life and relationships for their research participants. They can hear about the ways that memories and feelings shape people's perceptions, motivations and aspirations. And because of the versatility and flexibility of qualitative interviewing, researchers can respond and enquire further into complex, ambiguous and contradictory issues as their interview participants raise them. Such strengths have been argued to be beneficial for policymakers in understanding how and why a policy programme or service intervention may or may not work as intended, and what might be done to improve it or pursue a better alternative (e.g. Ford and Goger 2021).

We have seen from the discussion in this book that the qualitative interview method has been evolving, strengthening research interviewing practice, incorporating technological change and using visual and other methods within the interview to enhance the process of knowledge production (see Chapter 5). The method can provide depth and detail to the more general picture/viewpoint offered by quantitative social data, and so qualitative interviews can form a crucial part of complex multimodal studies, combining multiple qualitative methods or multiple qualitative and quantitative methods; in the longitudinal context when following participants through time, they can provide a way into uncovering complex processes of causality that (e.g. Treanor et al. 2021).

Kathleen Gerson and Sarah Damaske (2020) pose qualitative interviews as both a science and an art. Qualitative interviewing combines a systematic method and creative insight that enables social researchers to generate a range of evidence about social and mental processes, social patterns and trends, power dynamics and actions, life trajectories and links between macro-structures and meso-micro processes, and to build theoretical explanations of the relationship between social change and people's actions. One of the issues they and other commentators (e.g. Morse 2020) identify as a challenge for qualitative interviewers though is criticism of small samples. Indeed, the notion of 'big data' is a feature of the broader social research environment for qualitative interviewing thrown up by digitization and automated processes, along with access to secondary interview data.

Digital Change in the Research Environment

Change in the social research environment for qualitative interviewing has often been mediated by technological advances in equipment and software. Qualitative interviews can now be generated, represented and processed in digital form. Qualitative researchers are located in a broader research context where digitization has opened up expectations of larger data sets and faster automated analysis:

> The digital transformation of information and communication technologies means that qualitative researchers are not insulated from the changes that are opening up new efficiencies, larger data sets, quicker analysis, and new ways of answering important questions . . . [they] are not insulated from the trend towards digital data sets that can accumulate in richness, detail and size very significantly over short periods of time . . . qualitative researchers who have traditionally worked with small sample sizes may increasingly deal with larger and thicker digital data sets in a digital age. (Mills 2019: 9/32/33)

Extensive digital data, and its analysis, often is referred to as 'big data'. The term typically captures the unprecedented generation, aggregation and analysis of complex data, at great scale and speed. Big data includes digitally captured information from, for example, public administrative records, business transactions, internet and mobile technologies, locational data and their subjection to computational analytics through advanced automated data analytic methods. Enthusiasm about big data and its digital form, and the belief that 'big' provides 'better' information, has had an impact on expectations of how much data researchers should be collating. In the face of potential marginalization of qualitative research and interview testimonies by 'exploding data' (Flick 2019; Lanford et al. 2019), the idea of 'big qual' has begun to emerge. Big qual denotes the handling and analysis of large volumes of complex qualitative and qualitative longitudinal data, including working with multiple archived data sets. What constitutes the large volumes of big qual is subject to debate – How much interview data is big qual? (echoing the 'how many interviews is enough?' question we discussed in Chapter 6). On the one hand, there is a quantitative approach to big qual, posing it as crossing the threshold of a specific amount of research participants or number of interviews. For example, Rebecca Brower and colleagues (2019) define big qual as primary or secondary qualitative data from at least 100 participants being analysed by a team of researchers, while others have referred to various amounts of qualitative interview transcripts and other data (e.g. Fontaine et al. 2020; Vila-Henninger et al. 2022). On the other hand, there is a more particularistic and contextual approach to what constitutes big qual. Emma Davidson and colleagues (2019) understand big qual as an amount of interview data that is beyond the capacity of the researcher or research team involved to read through and analyse using standard in-depth qualitative analytic methods alone.

The vast quantities of individual and group interview data that can be generated from the pursuit of larger interview samples, and the proliferation of sophisticated computer-aided qualitative data analysis software (CAQDAS) that we looked at in Chapter 2, to manage faster analysis of more material, lead to questions about transcribing the extensive audio files for automated analytic processing. Manual transcription can be a time-consuming if worthwhile endeavour but may be nigh on impossible in the face of big qual data sets. Researchers have turned to automated methods to create 'good enough' transcripts of recorded audio material. The idea is that automated transcription software enables the production of a 'good enough' initial version of the interview transcript, which is then reviewed and amended by the researcher. This solution to turning audio into text, however, may raise ethical issues in addition to the conception of the nature of interviews that has already been noted in Chapter 2. Both cloud-based video conferencing services used for conducting interviews online and CAQDAS packages often have inbuilt transcription functions, which seems to be a useful automated answer to the audio-to-text workload. Concerns have been raised, however, about the privacy and security of this processing of data where a third party [the platform] is involved and may have access to what might be sensitive and person-identifiable material (e.g. Da Silva 2021).

Several of those contributors debating what constitutes big qual do so as researchers who have merged multiple qualitative interview data sets from several research projects into a large corpus for secondary analysis (Davidson et al. 2019; Vila-Henninger et al. 2022). Increasingly primary qualitative interview material is made available through archives for other researchers to use and undertake secondary analysis of a selected sub-sample, a full data set or merged data sets of interview transcripts. Examples of such repositories include the Henry A. Murray Research Archive and the Qualitative Data Repository (USA), the UK Data Archive and the Timescapes Archive (UK), the Irish Qualitative Data Archive (Ireland), the Finnish Social Science Data Archive (Finland), Qualiservice (Germany), Qualitative Data Archive (Poland) and the Australian Data Archive (Australia) (see also annotated bibliography). There are also oral history archives in many areas internationally, with audio recordings and interview transcripts. Guides to accessing and conducting secondary qualitative analysis of existing interview material provide assessments of the systematic processes, advantages and challenges of this form of research (e.g. Chatfield 2020; Hughes and Tarrant 2019; Largan and Morris 2019).

Philosophical Change in the Research Environment

Different philosophies and epistemologies offer different specifications on what constitutes legitimate knowledge and on the criteria that are used to establish that knowledge as credible. These issues are evident in the radical critique of interviewing debate that we introduced in Chapter 1 and referred to at various points throughout this book. They are reflected in the push towards qualitative researchers mirroring big data, and the challenge to interviews from big data, propelled by linked ideas of naturalism and empiricism. Big data is regarded as 'naturalistic' (rather than constructed digital traces), with researchers positioned as working with and analysing data that occurs independent of their practices and methods (e.g. social media). It has marshalled in a 'new era of empiricism', where it is contended that the sheer size of naturalistic information being generated and its subjection to automated analytic techniques can supposedly 'enable data to speak for themselves' as an objective form of knowing (Kitchin 2014). Such a decontextualized view of social life and people as knowable through the quantification abstracted from digital information – their datafication (Mejias and Couldry 2019) – sets itself against the complex social engagements between researchers and their research participants and attention to sociocultural context that comprise qualitative interviewing.

In direct contrast to a big data/datafication shaping understanding of qualitative interviews and data, stands an alternative philosophical presence in the research environment – the decolonization of research and Indigenous methodologies that we outlined in Chapter 2. Indeed, datafication can be understood as a new mode of data colonialism, a rationality where human life is appropriated and

> data can be continuously extracted from it for the benefit of particular (Western, but also increasingly global capitalist) interests. Instead of territories, natural resources, and enslaved labour, data colonialism appropriates social resources. (Mejias and Couldry 2019: 6)

The extractive view of what counts as legitimate knowledge and credible means of generating it through research that is implicit in big data and datafication as the best way of knowing is challenged by decoloniality. The notion of decolonization displaces datafication as the only framework for generating knowledge, and Indigenous philosophies and methodologies are non-extractive and non-essentializing ways of understanding, in the service of transformative research. Indigenous epistemologies provide qualitative interview researchers with a glimpse of another knowledge order beyond the mainstream for the framing of research and interviews. Vivetha Thambinathan and Elizabeth Anne Kinsella (2021), for example, propose a set of long-term decolonizing approaches that qualitative researchers can draw on (i) the exercise of critical reflexivity to examine their epistemological assumptions, positioning and research focus; (ii) reciprocity and respect for self-determination through inclusive collaboration across the research process; (iii) embracing and valuing 'Other(ed)' ways of knowing; and (iv) embodying a transformative praxis, opening up space, acknowledgement and legitimacy for decolonizing theory, values and practices in the wider research environment.

Interviewing per se, then, is not the main issue when considering the shifting research environment in which the method is located. Interviews are neutral tools in terms of being a talking method. Rather, at root of the debates and contestations around: the radical critique of interviews; changing technologies, the rise of datafication and emergence of big qual; and interest in transformative decolonization and Indigenous methodologies, is the philosophical and epistemological nature of qualitative interviews (Edwards and Holland 2020) – what they are and why they proceed as they do.

Conclusion

Throughout this book, we have provided information, suggestions and advice about qualitative interviews. Our basic approach can be summarized in a few points.

- The philosophical approach of a piece of research underpins understandings and leads to choices about:
  - ○ what interviews are and how they can be used,
  - ○ how the person being interviewed is positioned,
  - ○ the types of interview to use,
  - ○ the tools to use in the interview and
  - ○ how many people to interview.

- Attention must be paid to the social context of the interview and concomitant:

○ meanings and social and power relations intersecting in socio-spatial and time/place dimensions of interviews,
○ power and emotional dynamics that shape interviews.

In the final chapter, we hope to have brought encouragement to the aspiring qualitative interviewer that the method still has considerable mileage and much to offer social research but that we must, as in our interviews, be flexible and responsive in order to meet the increasing challenges that confront us in the changing social and research environment.

ANNOTATED BIBLIOGRAPHY

In this brief annotated bibliography, we provide references to a range of books and edited collections that provide good discussions of qualitative interviewing, followed by methods-related journals that can be consulted for articles about interviewing.

Books and Edited Collections

Most general social research textbooks cover qualitative interview methods, but there are a number of introductory texts, books, handbooks and edited collections that focus specifically on qualitative interviews. The fact that several of these have been updated and republished in new editions attests to their popularity and enduring relevance.

Brinkmann, S. and Kvale, S. (2015) *InterViews: Learning the Craft of Qualitative Research Interviewing*, 3rd edn, Thousand Oaks, CA, London and New Delhi: Sage.
As part of a general introduction to interviewing, the third edition of this influential book identifies enabling knowing through psychoanalytic research interview practice, with an emphasis on interviews as conversations. It covers aspects of interview research including intensive individual case studies; open and non-directive modes of interviewing; interpretation of meaning to allow for ambiguity and contradiction; temporal intertwining of past, present

and future; and emotional human interaction. An unusual feature of this edition is the internal debate boxes to provide a sense of the issues at stake.

Flick, U. (2021) *Doing Interview Research: The Essential How to Guide*, Thousand Oaks, CA, London and New Delhi: Sage.
An introductory, teaching text that takes you through a range of interviewing formats, including semi-structured and in-depth, individual and group, and in person and online. An interesting element that few textbooks cover is the inclusion of Indigenous approaches to interviews. There are practical exercises and supportive online case study resources to access.

Gubrium, J.F., Holstein, J.A., Marvasti, A.B. and McKinney, K.D. (eds) (2012) *The SAGE Handbook of Interview Research: The Complexity of the Craft*, 2nd edn, Thousand Oaks, CA, London and New Delhi: Sage.
This handbook is an updated comprehensive collection surveying a range of forms of interviews, with an emphasis on interviews as dynamic communicative encounters. The book is organized into parts with contributions about qualitative interviews that address context, methods, logistics, positionality, ethics and so on.

Gubrium, J.F. and Holstein, J.A. (eds) (2003) *Postmodern Interviewing*, Thousand Oaks, CA, London and New Delhi: Sage.
An influential collection of pieces concerned with postmodern interview practice. Contributions to the collection explore the way that the exchange between interviewer and interviewee/s – when, how and why questions are asked and stories constructed – is of significance. The collection as a whole conveys the variety of experimental possibilities of postmodern approaches for understanding and undertaking qualitative interviewing.

King, N. and Horrocks, C. (2019) *Interviews in Qualitative Research*, Thousand Oaks, CA, London and New Delhi: Sage.
A strength of this introductory book is that it discusses philosophies and explanation of concepts, alongside step-by-step practical advice about how to undertake various types of qualitative interviews in different settings and conditions. Phenomenological, discourse and narrative approaches receive particular attention.

Lareau, A. (2021) *Listening to People: A Practical Guide to Interviewing, Participant Observation, Data Analysis and Writing It All Up*, Chicago, IL: Chicago University Press.
This is an accessible and useful 'how to' book for novice researchers, covering interview-based and participant observation research and stressing the core importance of listening to our interviewees. Lareau provides pragmatic advice about preparing for and conducting interviews, as well as pitfalls to avoid, with a chapter devoted to commentary on extensive examples of interviews.

Merton, R.K., Fiske, M. and Kendall, P.L. (1990 [1956]) *The Focused Interview: A Manual of Problems and Procedures*, New York: Free Press/Macmillan.
Chapter 7 of this revised and updated version of Merton's classic 1956 text on qualitative interviewing guides the reader through the technique of group interviews specifically. In particular, Merton argues that a good focus group interview aims to cover range, specificity, depth and context for a topic through group interaction. The discussion of the advantages and disadvantages of the method remains telling.

Roulston, K. (2022) *Interviewing: A Guide to Theory and Practice*, London: Sage
An updated introductory book with a strong emphasis on the connection between theory and interview methods. The book also covers designing interview studies, individual and group interviews, and pays particular attention to the practice of reflexivity.

Rubin, H.J. and Rubin, I.S. (2011) *Qualitative Interviewing: The Art of Hearing Data*, 3rd edn, Thousand Oaks, CA, London and New Delhi: Sage.
This introductory text on interviewing stresses the importance of listening. Rubin and Rubin cover the stages prior to and following on the interview itself, using empirical examples to illustrate and demonstrate points.

Salmons, J. (2014) *Qualitative Online Interviews: Strategies, Design and Skills*, 2nd edn, Thousand Oaks, CA, London and New Delhi: Sage.
This book addresses readers as both research practitioners and teachers of research methods. It is useful to dip into for ideas about

the gamut of online interviews, or e-interview as Salmons terms it, and their relationship to time and presence: how they can be mixed with other methods of research, how to use them and their strengths and limitations. There is also a companion website with study tools and resources.

Spradley, J. P. (1979) *The Ethnographic Interview*, New York: Holt, Rinehart and Winston.
This is a classic methods text that stresses the search for meaning that people make of their lives through investigating tacit cultural knowledge and processes. Spradley presents a systematic, step-by-step, approach to ethnographic interviewing from locating an informant through to writing up. His categorization of types of questions and probes has been very influential.

Journals

There are several peer-refereed journals addressing various methodological approaches and techniques, including journals specializing in qualitative methods.

Forum: Qualitative Social Research/ Forum Qualitative Sozialforschung

This journal publishes a diverse mix of substantive and methods-based articles on aspects of qualitative research, including many addressing aspects of interviewing, and it is available at www.qualitative-research.net/index.php/fqs

International Journal of Qualitative Methods

Assorted aspects of interviewing with an emphasis on advances, innovations and insights into qualitative and mixed methods are a feature of this journal. It is available at https://journals.sagepub.com/home/ijq

International Journal of Social Research Methodology

Qualitative interviews in various forms are a recurrent topic of articles in standard issues of this journal as well as themed sections and special issues, which are available at https://www.tandfonline.com/loi/tsrm20

Qualitative Inquiry

This journal publishes articles concerned with emancipatory and experimental approach to qualitative research, including interviews. It is available at https://journals.sagepub.com/home/qix

Qualitative Report

A multidisciplinary qualitative research journal that publishes a range of forms of articles on the gamut of research methods, including interview methods. It is available at https://nsuworks.nova.edu/tqr/

Qualitative Research

This methodological journal often contains long-form and short-form pieces on interviewing from an interpretive perspective in particular and is available at https://journals.sagepub.com/home/qrj

Qualitative Research Journal

A journal with a focus on the theory and practice of qualitative research across the human sciences. It is available at https://www.emeraldgrouppublishing.com/journal/qrj

Online Resources

The ESRC National Centre for Research Methods provides methodological training and resources on core and advanced research methods. They provide downloadable video, podcast, quick guides and working paper resources, including on qualitative interviewing and as part of mixed and multimodal methods. They are available at www.ncrm.ac.uk/

Several research centres have produced basic information sheets on qualitative interviewing, such as the following:

Department of Sociology at Harvard University: https://sociology. fas.harvard.edu/files/sociology/files/interview_strategies.pdf

University of Kansas Community Tool Box: https://ctb.ku.edu/en/ table-of-contents/assessment/assessing-community-needs-and-resources/conduct-interviews/main

Oxfam Policy and Practice: https://policy-practice.oxfam.org/ resources/conducting-semi-structured-interviews-252993/

Archived Qualitative Interview Data for Secondary Analysis and Teaching

Increasingly qualitative interview data from projects is being archived and made available to researchers for secondary analysis electronically. The archives may also provide resources for teaching qualitative interviewing and secondary interview analysis. Here are some examples of social science archives with qualitative interview holdings that are available for search, download and analysis online:

Henry A. Murray Research Archive: https://murray.harvard.edu/

Although the Murray archive is located in Harvard's Institute for Quantitative Social Science, it houses a number of qualitative interview projects in its 'dataverse'. There is a particular emphasis on data holdings about women's lives and issues.

Irish Qualitative Data Archive: https://www.maynoothuniversity.ie/iqda

The Irish archive holds qualitative social science data generated in or about Ireland, including oral histories as well as contemporary qualitative interview material. They provide information from demonstrator secondary analysis projects as well as bespoke guidance for specific secondary analysis projects.

Timescapes Qualitative Longitudinal Data Archive: https://timescapes-archive.leeds.ac.uk/

The Timescapes Archive specializes in qualitative longitudinal research data sets. It is one of the first archives specifically to hold such data for reuse. A range of 'how to' guides and resources are available to support secondary analysis of the Timescapes deposits, and there are also teaching resources on working with large amounts of qualitative interview data.

UK Data Service: https://ukdataservice.ac.uk/ learning-hub/qualitative-data/

The UK Data Service archives data from a range of social science research projects, including historical and recent qualitative research projects using interview and other qualitative methods. It provides information about reusing qualitative data, searching for the archive for relevant projects and resources for teaching interview and other qualitative methods.

REFERENCES

Aarsand, L. and Aarsand, P. (2019) 'Framing and switches at the outset of qualitative research interviews', *Qualitative Research* 19(6): 635–652.

Ahmed, S. (2017) *Living a Feminist Life*, Durham, NC: Duke University Press.

Alastalo, M. (2008) 'The history of social research methods', in P. Alasuutari, L. Bickman and J. Brannen (eds) *The SAGE Handbook of Social Research Methods*, 26–41, London: Sage.

Andrews, M. (2021) 'Quality indicators in narrative research', *Qualitative Research in Psychology* 18(3): 353–368.

Atkinson, C. (2019) 'Ethical complexities in participatory childhood research: Rethinking the "least adult role"', *Childhood* 26(2): 186–201.

Atkinson, P. and Sampson, C. (2019) 'Narrative stability in interview accounts', *International Journal of Social Research Methodology* 22(1): 55–66.

Atkinson, P. and Silverman, D. (1997) 'Kundera's immortality: The interview society and the invention of self', *Qualitative Inquiry* 3(3): 304–325.

Aujla, W. (2020) 'Using a vignette in qualitative research to explore police perspectives of a sensitive topic: "Honor"-based crimes and forced marriages', *International Journal of Qualitative Methods* 19: 1–10.

Ayrton, R. (2019) 'The micro-dynamics of power and performance in focus groups: An example from discussions on national identity with the South Sudanese diaspora in the UK', *Qualitative Research* 19(3): 323–339.

Back, L. (2010) *Broken Devices and New Opportunities: Re-Imagining the Tools of Qualitative Research*, National Centre for Research Methods Working Paper 08/10. Online publication accessed 6.4.12: http://eprints.ncrm.ac.uk/1579/1/0810_broken_devices_Back.pdf.

Baker, S.E. and Edwards, R. (eds) (2012) *How Many Qualitative Interviews Is Enough? Expert Voices and Early Career Reflections on Sampling and Cases in Qualitative Research*, National Centre for Research Methods Review Paper. Online publication accessed 27.3.11: http://eprints.ncrm.ac.uk/2273/4/how_many_interviews.pdf.

Bashir, N. (2020) 'The qualitative researcher: The flip side of the research encounter with vulnerable people', *Qualitative Research* 20(5): 667–683.

Bateman, J., Wildfeuer, J. and Hiippalla, T. (2017) *Multimodality: Foundations Research and Analysis: A Problem-Oriented Introduction*, Berlin: De Gruyter.

Bazeley, P. (2018) '"Mixed methods in my bones": Transcending the qualitative-quantitative divide', *International Journal of Multiple Research Approaches* 10(1): 334–341.

Becker, H.S. (1967) 'Whose side are we on?', *Social Problems* 14(3): 239–247.

Bell, C. (1978) 'Studying the locally powerful: Personal reflections on a research career', in C. Bell and S. Cencel (eds) *Inside the Whale*, 14–40, Sydney: Pergamon.

Bengtsson, T.T. and Fynbo, L. (2017) 'Analysing the significance of silence in qualitative interviewing: Questioning and shifting power relations', *Qualitative Research* 18(1): 19–35.

Bennett, B., Maar, M., Manitowabi, D., Moeke-Pickering, T., Trudeau-Pettier, D. and Trudeau, S. (2019) 'The Gaataabing visual research method: A culturally safe Anishinaabek transformation of photovoice', *International Journal of Qualitative Methods* 18: 1–12.

Bergmann Blix, S. and Wettergren, Å. (2015) 'The emotional labour of gaining and maintaining access to the field', *Qualitative Research* 15(6): 688–704.

Bernard, H.R. (2000) *Social Research Methods: Qualitative and Quantitative Approaches*, Thousand Oaks, CA, London and New Delhi: Sage.

Bezzini, R. (2017) 'On interviewing partners in mixed couples together: Performance, meta-communication and positionality', *Romanian Journal of Population Studies* 11(1): 7–21.

Blackstone, A. (2019) *Social Research: Qualitative and Quantitative Methods*, 2nd edn, Nyack, NY: Flat World Knowledge.

Blaikie, N. (2018) 'Confounding issues related to determining sample size in qualitative research', *International Journal of Social Research Methodology* 21(5): 615–641.

Blaikie, N. and Priest, J. (2019) *Designing Social Research: The Logic of Anticipation*, Cambridge: Polity.

Braun, V. and Clarke, V. (2021) 'To saturate or not to saturate? Questioning data saturation as a useful concept for thematic analysis and sample size rationales', *Qualitative Research in Sport, Exercise and Health* 13(2): 201–216.

Briggs, C.L. (2003) 'Interviewing, power/knowledge, and social inequality', in J.F. Gubrium and J.A. Holstein (eds) *Postmodern Interviewing*, 243–54, London: Sage.

Brinkmann, S. and Kvale, S. (2015) *InterViews: Learning the Craft of Qualitative Research Interviewing*, 3rd edn, Los Angeles, CA and London: Sage Publications.

Brinkmann, S. and Kvale, S. (2018) *Doing Interviews*, 2nd edn, London and Thousand Oaks, CA: Sage.

Britton, J. (2020) 'Being an insider and outsider: Whiteness as a key dimension of difference', *Qualitative Research* 20(3): 340–354.

Brower, R.L., Jones, T.B., Osborne-Lampkin, L., Hu, S. and Park-Gaghan, T.J. (2019) 'Big qual: Defining and debating qualitative inquiry for large data sets', *International Journal of Qualitative Methods* 18: 1–10.

Brown, N. (2019) 'Identity boxes: Using materials and metaphors to elicit experiences', *International Journal of Social Research Methodology* 22(5): 487–501.

Bryman, A. (2019) *Social Research Methods*, 4th edn, Oxford: Oxford University Press.

Buchanan, D. and Warwick, I. (2021) 'First do no harm: Using "ethical triage" to minimise causing harm when undertaking educational research among vulnerable participants', *Journal of Further and Higher Education* 45(8): 1090–1103.

Burgess, R.G. (1984) *In the Field: An Introduction to Field Research*, London: Allen & Unwin.

Byrne, A.-L., McLellan, S., Willis, E., Curnow, V., Harvey, C., Brown, J. and Hegney, D. (2021) 'Yarning as an interview method for non-Indigenous clinicians and health researchers', *Qualitative Health Research* 31(7): 1345–1357.

Chamberlayne, P., Bornat, J. and Wengraf, T. (2000) *The Turn to Biographical Methods in Social Science: Comparative Issues and Examples*, London: Routledge.

Chansky, R.A., Powell, K.M. and Trần, Đ. (2021) 'A necessary tension: Editors, editing and oral history for social justice', *The Oral History Review* 48(2): 258–272.

Chatfield, S.L. (2020) 'Recommendations for secondary analysis of qualitative data', *The Qualitative Report* 25(3): 833–842.

Chen, A.T. (2018) 'Timeline drawing and the online scrapbook: Two visual elicitation techniques for a richer exploration of illness journey', *International Journal of Qualitative Methods* 17(1): 1–13.

Chen, J. and Neo, P. (2019) 'Texting the waters: An assessment of focus groups conducted via the WhatsApp smartphone messaging application', *Methodological Innovations* 12(3): 1–10.

Chilisa, B. (2019) *Indigenous Research Methodologies*, 2nd edn, Los Angeles, CA and London: Sage.

Christopher, E. (2021) 'Capturing conflicting accounts of domestic labour: The household portrait as a methodology', *Sociological Research Online* 26(3): 451–468.

Clemens, R.F. and Lincoln, Y.S. (2020) 'Ethnography and public scholarship: Ethical obligations, tensions and opportunities', *Cultural Studies – Critical Methodologies* 20(5): 383–388.

Corbin, J. and Strauss, A. (2014) *Basics of Qualitative Research: Techniques and Procedures for Developing Grounded Theory*, 4th edn, London: Sage.

Cottingham, M.D. and Erickson, R.J. (2020) 'Capturing emotion with audio diaries', *Qualitative Research* 20(5): 549–564.

Crawley, S.L. (2012) 'Autoethnography as feminist self-interview', in J.F. Gubrium, J.A. Holstein, A.B. Marvasti and K.D. McKinney (eds) *The SAGE Handbook of Interview Research: The Complexity of the Craft*, 2nd edn, pp. 143–160, Thousand Oaks, CA: Sage.

Culpepper, M.K. and Gauntlett, D. (2021) 'Inviting everyday creators to make, think and talk', *Thinking Skills and Creativity* 42. https://doi.org/10.1016/j.tsc.2021.100933.

Dahlin, E. (2021) 'Email interviews: A guide to research design and implementation', *International Journal of Qualitative Methods* 20: 1–10.

Dang Vu, H.N. (2021) 'When cheap talk is not that cheap – Interviewing the super-rich about illegal wildlife consumption', *International Journal of Social Research Methodology*. https://www.tandfonline.com/doi/full/10.1080/13645579.2021.1904117.

Da Silva, J. (2021) 'Producing "good enough" automated transcripts securely: Extending Bokhove and Downey (2018) to address security concerns', *Methodological Innovations* 14(1): 1–11.

Davidson, E., Edwards, R., Jamieson, L. and Weller, S. (2019) 'Big data, qualitative style: A breadth-and-depth method for working with large amounts of secondary qualitative data', *Quality & Quantity* 53: 363–376.

Declercq, J. and Ayala, R. (2017) 'Examining "elite" power dynamics in informant-research relations and its impact on ethnographic data construction: A case study from pharmaceutical health communication', *International Journal of Qualitative Methods* 16: 1–12.

Denzin, N.K. (2010) *The Qualitative Manifesto: A Call to Arms*, New York: Routledge.

Denzin, N.K. and Lincoln, Y.S. (2017) 'Introduction: The discipline and practice of qualitative research', in N.K. Denzin and Y.S. Lincoln (eds) *The SAGE Handbook of Qualitative Research*, 5th edn, Los Angeles, CA and London: Sage.

Di Feliciantonio, C. (2021) '(Un)ethical boundaries: Critical reflections on what we are (not) supposed to do', *The Professional Geographer* 73(3): 496–503.

Donne, M.D., DeLuca, J., Pleskach, P., Bromson, C., Mosley, M.P., Perez, E.T., Mathews, S.G., Stephenson, R. and Frye, V. (2017) 'Barriers to and facilitators of help-seeking behaviour among men who experience sexual violence', *American Journal of Men's Health* 12(2): 189–201.

Drabble, L., Trocki, K.F., Salcedo, B., Walker, P.C. and Korcha, R.A. (2016) 'Conducitng qualitative interviews by telephone: Lessons learned from a study of alcohol use among sexual minorityand heterosexual women', *Qualitative Social Work* 15(1): 118–133.

Donne, M.D., DeLuca, J., Pleskach, P., Bromson, C., Mosley, M.P., Perez, E.T., Mathews, S.G., Stephenson, R. and Frye, V. (2017) 'Barriers to and facilitators of help-seeking behaviour among men who experience sexual violence', *American Journal of Men's Health* 12(2): 189–201.

Doucet, A. (2001) '"You see the need perhaps more clearly than I have": Exploring gendered processes of domestic responsibility', *Journal of Family Issues* 22: 328–357.

Doucet, A. and Mauthner, N. (2008) 'Qualitative interviewing and feminist research', in P. Alasuutari, L. Bickman and J. Brannen (eds) *The SAGE Handbook of Social Research Methods*, 328–43, London: Sage.

Draucker, C.B., Martsolf, D.S. and Poole, C. (2009) 'Developing protocols for research on sensitive topics', *Archives of Psychiatric Nursing* 23(5): 343–350.

Edwards, R. and Holland, J. (2020) 'Reviewing challenges and the future for qualitative interviewing', *International Journal of Social Research Methodology* 23(5): 581–592.

Elliott, A. (2015) *Psychoanalytic Theory: An Introduction*, 3rd edn, Basingstoke: Palgrave Macmillan.

Emmel, N. (2013) *Sampling and Choosing Cases in Qualitative Research*, London: Sage.

Finch, J. (1987) 'The vignette technique in survey research', *Sociology* 21: 105–114.

Finlay, J.M. and Bowman, J.A. (2017) 'Geographies on the move: A practical and theoretical approach to the mobile interview', *The Professional Geographer* 69(2): 263–274.

Flick, U. (2019) 'The concept of qualitative data: Challenges in neoliberal times for qualitative inquiry', *Qualitative Inquiry* 25(8): 713–720.

Fontaine, C.M., Baker, A.C., Zabhloul, T.H. and Carlson, M. (2020) 'Clinical data mining with the listening guide: An approach to narrative big qual', *International Journal of Qualitative Methods* 19: 1–13.

Ford, T.M. and Goger, A. (2021) *The value of qualitative data for advancing equity in policy*, Brookings Institute. https://www.brookings.edu/research/value-of-qualitative-data-for-advancing-equity-in-policy/.

Fox, N.J. and Alldred, P. (2018) '*New materialism*', in P.A. Atkinson, S. Delamont, M.A. Hardy and M. Williams (eds) *The SAGE Encyclopedia of Research Methods*, Los Angeles, CA and London: Sage.

Freire, P. (2018) *Pedagogy of the Oppressed: 50th Anniversary Edition*, London and New York: Bloomsbury Academic.

Gagnon, M., Jacob, J.D. and McCabe, J. (2015) 'Locating the qualitative interview: Reflecting on space and place in nursing research', *Journal of Research in Nursing* 20(3): 203–215.

Galam, R.G. (2015) 'Gender, reflexivity, and positionality in male research in one's own community with Filipino seafarers' wives', *Forum: Qualitative Social Research* 16(3): Art. 13. http://nbn-resolving.de/urn:nbn:de:0114-fqs1503139.

Gerson, K. and Damaske, S. (2020) *The Science and Art of Interviewing*, New York: Oxford University Press.

Gibbs, G.R. (2018) *Analyzing Qualitative Data*, London: Sage.

Giddens, A. (2011) *Runaway World: How Globalisation is Reshaping our Lives*, 2nd edn, Abingdon: Routledge.

Glaser, B.G. and Strauss, A. (1967) *The Discovery of Grounded Theory: Strategies for Qualitative Research*, Chicago, IL: Aldine.

Goffman, A. (2014) *On the Run: Fugitive Life in an American City*, Chicago, IL: University of Chicago Press.

Golombisky, K. (2018) 'Feminist methodology', in L.Z. Leslie (ed) *Communication Research Methods in Postmodern Culture: A Revisionist Approach*, 2nd edn, 172–96, New York: Routledge.

Graham, E. (2022) 'The ethnographer unbared: Honoring hatred in uncomfortable terrains', *Forum Qualitative Sozialforschung/Forum: Qualitative Social Research* 23(1): Art. 9. http://dx.doi.org/10.17169/fqs-23.1.3857.

Granek, L. (ed) (2017) 'Special section: Emotional engagement', *Qualitative Psychology* 4(3): 281–352.

Griffin, G. (ed) (2018) *Cross-Cultural Interviewing: Feminist Experiences and Reflections*, Abingdon: Routledge.

Gubrium, J.F. and Holstein, J.A. (2003a) 'From the individual interview to the interview society', in J.F. Gubrium and J.A. Holstein (eds) *Postmodern Interviewing*, London: Sage.

Gubrium, J.F. and Holstein, J.A. (eds) (2003b) *Postmodern Interviewing*, London: Sage.

Hammersley, M. and Atkinson, P. (2019) *Ethnography: Principles in Practice*, 4th edn, Abingdon: Routledge.

Harper, D. (2012) *Visual Sociology*, London and New York: Routledge.

Henwood, K., Shirani, F. and Finn, M. (2011) '"So you think we've moved, changed, the representation got more what?" Methodological and analytical reflections on visual (photo-elicitation) methods used in the Men as Fathers study', in P. Reavey (ed) *Visual Methods in Psychology: Using and Interpreting Images in Qualitative Research*, 330–45, London: Routledge.

Hepburn, A. and Boden, G.B. (2017) *Transcribing for Social Research*, London: Sage.

Herz, A. and Altissimo, A. (2021) 'Understanding the structures of transnational youth im/mobility: A qualitative network analysis', *Global Networks* 12(3): 500–512.

Herzog, H. (2012) 'Interview location and its social meaning', in J.F. Gubrium, J.A. Holstein, A.B. Marvasti and K.D. McKinney (eds) *The SAGE Handbook of Interview Research: The Complexity of the Craft*, 2nd edn, 207–18, Los Angeles, CA: Sage.

Hesse-Biber, S. (2015) 'Introduction: Navigating a turbulent research landscape: Working the boundaries, tensions, diversity, and contradictions of multimethod and mixed methods inquiry', in S.M. Hesse-Biber and R.B. Johnson (eds) *The Oxford Handbook of Multimethod and Mixed Methods Research Inquiry*, pp. xxxiii–liii, Oxford: Oxford University Press.

Hesse-Biber, S. (2021) *Handbook of Feminist Research: Theory and Praxis*, 2nd edn, Thousand Oaks, CA: Sage.

Hesse-Biber, S., Rodriguez, D. and Frost, N.A. (2015) 'A qualitatively-driven approach to multimethod and mixed-methods research', in S.M. Hesse-Biber and R.B. Johnson (eds) *The Oxford Handbook of Multimethod and Mixed Methods Research Inquiry*, pp. 3–20, Oxford: Oxford University Press.

Holstein, J.A. and Gubrium, J.F. (2016) 'Narrative practice and the active interview', in D. Silverman (ed) *Qualitative Research*, 4th edn, London and New York: Sage Publications.

Holtan, A., Strandbu, A. and Eriksen, S.H. (2014) 'When emotions count in construction of interview data', *Nordic Social Work Research* 4(2): 99–112.

Howlett, M. (2021) 'Looking at the "field" through a Zoom lens: Methodological reflections on conducting online research during a global pandemic', *Qualitative Research*. https://journals.sagepub.com/doi/pdf/10.1177/1468794120985691.

Hughes, J., Hughes, K., Sykes, G. and Wright, K. (2020) 'Beyond performative talk: Critical observations on the radical critique of reading interview data', *International Journal of Social Research Methodology* 23(5): 547–563. http://doi.org/10.1080/13645579.2020.1766757.

Hughes, K. and Tarrant, A. (eds) (2019) *Qualitative Secondary Analysis*, Los Angeles, CA: Sage.

Humphreys, L. (1970) *Tearoom Trade: Impersonal Sex in Public Places*, London: Duckworth.

Humphries, B., Mertens, D.M. and Truman, C. (2000) 'Arguments for an "emancipatory" research paradigm', in C. Truman, D.M. Mertens and B. Humphries (eds) *Research and Inequality*, 1–21, London and New York: Routledge.

Islam, M. (2020) 'Reflection note: Confessions of a Muslim researcher – Considering identity in research', *International Journal of Social Research Methodology* 23(5): 509–515.

Jaggar, A. (1989) 'Love and knowledge: Emotion in feminist epistemology', in S. Bordo and A. Jaggar (eds) *Gender/Body/Knowledge: Feminist Reconstructions of Being and Knowing*, 145–70, New Brunswick, NJ: Rutgers University Press.

Jen, S., Zhou, Y. and Jeong, M. (2020) '"You'll see": Younger women interviewing older women in qualitative research', *Journal of Gerontological Social Work* 63(8): 753–767.

Jenkins, N., Bloor, M., Fischer, J., Berney, L. and Neale, J. (2010) 'Putting it in context: The use of vignettes in qualitative interviewing', *Qualitative Research* 10(2): 175–198.

Jenks, C.J. (2011) *Transcribing Talk and Interaction: Issues in the Representation of Communication Data*, Amsterdam and Philadelphia, PA: John Benjamins.

Jewitt, C., Bezemer, J. and O'Halloran, K. (2016) *Introducing Multimodality*, London: Routledge.

Kaufman, K., Peil, C. and Bork-Hüffer, T. (2021) 'Producing in situ data from a distance with mobile instant messaging interviews (MIMIs): Examples from the COVID-19 pandemic', *International Journal of Qualitative Methods* 20: 1–14.

Kee, K.F. and Schrock, A.R. (2019) 'Telephone interviewing as a qualitaiatie ethodology for researching cyberinfrastructure and virutal organisations', in J. Hunsinger, M. Allen and L. Klastrup (eds) *Second International Handbook of Internet Research*, pp. 352–365, Dordrecht: Springer.

Keightley, E., Pickering, M. and Allett, N. (2012) 'The self-interview: A new method in social science research', *International Journal of Social Research Methodology* 15(6): 507–521.

Kitchin, R. (2014) 'Big data, new epistemologies and paradigm shifts', *Big Data and Society* 1(1): 1–12.

Kitzinger, J. (2005) 'Focus group research: Using group dynamics to explore perceptions, experiences and understandings', in I. Holloway (ed) *Qualitative Research in Health Care*, pp. 56–69, Maidenhead: Open University Press.

Klein, M. and Milner, R.J. (2019) 'The use of body-mapping in interpretiative phenomenological analyses: A methodological discussion', *International Journal of Social Research Methodology* 22(5) 533–543.

Klykken, F.H. (2021) 'Implementing continuous consent in qualitative research', *Qualitative Research*. https://journals.sagepub.com/doi/full/10.1177/14687941211014366.

Kovach, M. (2019) 'Conversational method in Indigenous research', *First Peoples Child & Family Review [Special edition]* 14(1): 123–137.

Lancaster, K. (2017) 'Confidentiality, anonymity and power relations in elite interviewing: Conducting qualitative policy research in a politicised domain', *International Journal of Social Research Methodology* 20(1): 93–103.

Lanford, M., Tierney, W.G. and Lincoln, Y. (2019) 'The art of life history: Novel approaches, future direction', *Qualitative Inquiry* 25(5): 459–463.

Largan, C. and Morris, T. (2019) *Qualitative Secondary Research: A Step-By-Step Guide*, Los Angeles, CA: Sage.

Lawton, K. (2018) 'He said, she said, we said: Ethical issues in conducting dyadic interviews', in R. Iphofen and M. Tolich (eds) *The SAGE Handbook of Qualitative Research Ethics*, 133–47, London and New York: Sage Publications.

Lefkowich, M. (2019) 'When women study men: Gendered implications for qualitative research', *International Journal of Qualitative Methods* 18: 1–9.

Letherby, G. (2003) *Feminist Research in Theory and Practice*, Buckingham: Open University Press.

Linn, S. (2021) 'Solicited diary methods with urban refugee women: Ethical and practical considerations', *Area* 53(3): 454–463.

Lobe, B. and Morgan, D.L. (2021) 'Assessing the effectiveness of video-based interviewing: A systematic comparison of video-conferencing based dyadic interviews and focus groups', *International Journal of Social Research Methodology* 24(3): 301–312.

Lohmeyer, B.A. (2019) '"Keen as fuck": Youth participation in qualitative research as "parallel projects"', *Qualitative Research* 20(1): 39–55.

Luker, K. (2008) *Salsa Dancing into the Social Sciences: Research in an Age of Info-Glut*, Cambridge, MA: Harvard University Press.

Mahtani, M. (2012) 'Not the same difference: Notes on mixed-race methodologies', in R. Edwards, S. Ali, C. Caballero and M. Song (eds) *International Perspectives on Racial and Ethnic Mixedness and Mixing*, 156–68, Abingdon: Routledge.

Malinowski, B. (1922) *Argonauts of the Western Pacific: An Account of Native Enterprise and Adventure in the Archipelagoes of Melanesian New Guinea*, New York: Dutton.

Marn, T.M. and Wolegemuth, J.R. (2017) 'Purposeful entanglements: A new materialist analysis of transformative interviews', *Qualitative Inquiry* 23(5): 365–374.

Mason, J. (2006) *Six Strategies for Mixing Methods and Linking Data in Social Science Research*, Real Life Methods NCRM Node Working Paper. Online publication accessed 31.3.13: www.socialsciences

.manchester.ac.uk/morgancentre/realities/wps/4–2006–07-rlm-mason.
pdf.

Mason, J. (2018) *Qualitative Researching*, 3rd edn, London: Sage.

Mauthner, N.S. and Parry, O. (2009) 'Qualitative data preservation
and sharing in the social sciences: On whose philosophical terms?',
Australian Journal of Social Issues 44(3): 289–305.

Mao, J. and Feldman, E. (2018) 'Class matters: Interviewing across
social class boundaries', *International Journal of Social Research
Methodology* 22(2): 125–137.

Marshall, S.A., Hudson, H.K. and Stigar, L.V. (2020) 'Perceptions of a
school-based sexuality education curriculum: Findings from focus
groups with parents and teens in a Southern state', *The Health
Educator* 52(1): 37–51.

Maxwell, J.A. (2012) *A Realist Approach to Qualitative Research*, Los
Angeles, CA: Sage.

McClelland, S. (2017) 'Vulnerable listening: Possibilities and challenges of
doing qualitative research', *Qualitative Psychology* 4(3): 338–352.

McCusker, S. (2020) 'Everybody's monkey is important: LEGO® Serious
Play® as a methodology for enabling equality of voice within diverse
groups', *International Journal of Research and Method in Education*
43(2): 146–162.

McDonnell, L., Scott, S. and Dawson, M. (2016) 'A multi dimensional
view? Evaluating the different and combined contributions of diaries
and interviews in an exploration of asexual identities and intimacies',
Qualitative Research 17(5): 520–536.

McGrath, L., Mullarkey, S. and Reavey, P. (2019) 'Building visual worlds:
Using maps in qualitative research in affect and emotion', *Qualitative
Research in Psychology* 17(1): 75–97.

McLaughlin, H., Uggen, C. and Blackstone, A. (2012) 'Sexual harassment,
workplace authority, and the paradox of power', *American
Sociological Review* 77(4): 625–647.

Mead, G.H. (1935) *Mind, Self and Society*, Chicago, IL: University of
Chicago Press.

Mejias, U.A. and Couldry, N. (2019) 'Datafication', *Internet Policy
Review* 8(4). https://policyreview.info/pdf/policyreview-2019-4-1428
.pdf.

Mertens, D.M. (2009) *Transformative Research and Evaluation*, New
York and London: The Guildford Press.

Mellor, J., Ingram, N., Abrahams, J. and Beedell, P. (2014) 'Class matters
in the interview setting? Positionality, situatedness and class', *British
Educational Research Journal* 40(1): 135–149.

Miller, R.L. (2000) *Researching Life Stories and Family Histories*,
London: Sage.

Miller, T. and Boulton, M. (2007) 'Changing constructions of informed consent: Qualitative research and complex social worlds', *Social Science & Medicine* 65(11): 2199–2211.

Mills, C. Wright (1959) *The Sociological Imagination*, New York: Oxford University Press.

Mills, K.A. (2019) *Big Data for Qualitative Research*, Abingdon and New York: Routledge.

Mizock, L., Harkins, D. and Morant, R. (2011) 'Researcher interjecting in qualitative race research', *Forum: Qualitative Social Research* 12(2): Art. 13. http://nbn-resolving.de/urn:nbn:de:0114-fqs1102134.

Moran, R.J. and Asquith, N.L. (2020) 'Understanding the vicarious trauma and emotional labour of criminological research', *Methodological Innovations* 13(2): 1–11.

Morgan, D.L. (1997) *Focus Groups as Qualitative Research*, 2nd edn, Thousand Oaks, CA: Sage.

Morgan, D.L. (2018) *Basic and Advanced Focus Groups*, New York: Sage Publications.

Morse, J.M. (2015) 'Issues in qualitatively-driven mixed methods designs: Walking through a mixed methods project', in S.M. Hesse-Biber and R.B. Johnson (eds) *The Oxford Handbook of Multimethod and Mixed Methods Research Inquiry*, 206–22, Oxford: Oxford University Press.

Morse, J. (2020) 'The changing face of qualitative inquiry', *International Journal of Qualitative Methods* 19: 1–7.

Mott, R., Tummons, J., Simonsen, J. and Vandermau, R. (2021) 'Photo elicitation: Useful supplemental tool for qualitative interviews with youths', *The Journal of Extension* 58(1). https://tigerprints.clemson.edu/joe/vol58/iss1/4.

Mukumbang, F.C., Marchal, B., Van Belle, S. and van Whyk, B. (2019) 'Using the realist interview approach to maintain theoretical awareness in realist studies', *Qualitative Research* 20(4): 485–515.

Nind, M. (2014) *What is Inclusive Research*, London and New York: Bloomsbury Academic.

Nind, M. (2020) *Inclusive Research Methods*, London: Bloomsbury Academic.

Nordstrom, S.N. (2015) 'Not so innocent anymore: Making recording devices matter in qualitative interviews', *Qualitative Inquiry* 21(4): 388–401.

Oakley, A. (1981) 'Interviewing women: A contradiction in terms', in H. Roberts (ed) *Doing Feminist Research*, 30–61, London: Routledge.

O'Neill, M. and Roberts, B. (2020) *Walking Methods: Research on the Move*, Abingdon: Routledge.

Orlans, H. (1971) 'The political uses of social research', *The Annals of the American Academy of Political and Social Science* 394: 28–35.

Ozano, K. and Khatri, R. (2018) 'Reflexivity, positionality and power in cross-cultural participatory action research with research assistants in rural Cambodia', *Educational Action Research* 26(2): 190–204.

Payne, G. (ed) (2013) *Social Divisions*, 3rd edn, Basingstoke: Palgrave Macmillan.

Park, R. and Burgess, E. (1925) *The City*, Chicago, IL: University of Chicago Press.

Parker, C., Scott, S. and Geddes, A. (2019) 'Snowball sampling', in P. Atkinson, S. Delamont, A. Cernat, J.W. Sakshaug and R.A. Williams (eds) *SAGE Research Methods Foundations*. https://www.doi.org/10.4135/9781526421036831710.

Patton, M.Q. (2017) *Qualitative Research and Evaluation Methods*, 5th edn, London: Sage.

Payne, G. (ed) (2013) *Social Divisions*, 3rd edn, Basingstoke: Palgrave Macmillan.

Pearce, L.D. (2015) 'Thinking outside the Q boxes: Further motivating a mixed research perspective', in S.M. Hesse-Biber and R.B. Johnson (eds) *The Oxford Handbook of Multimethod and Mixed Methods Research Inquiry*, pp. 42–56, Oxford: Oxford University Press.

Peta, C., Wengraf, T. and McKenzie, J. (2019) 'Facilitating the voice of disabled women: The biographic narrative interpretive method (BNIM) in action', *Contemporary Social Science* 14(3–4): 515–527.

Ponizovsky-Bergelson, Y., Dayan, Y., Wahle, N. and Roer-Strier, D. (2019) 'A qualitative interview with young children: What encourages or inhibits young children's participation?', *International Journal of Qualitative Methods* 18: 1–19.

Reissman, C.K. (2007) *Narrative Methods for the Human Sciences*, Los Angeles, CA: Sage Publications.

Rodriguez, K.L., Broyles, L.M., Mitchell, M.A., Wieland, M.E., True, G. and Gordon, A.J. (2019) '"Build a bridge so you can cross it": A photo-elicitation study of health and wellness among homeless and marginally housed veterans', *The Qualitative Report* 24(2): 371–394. https://nsuworks.nova.edu/tqr/vol24/iss2/14.

Rogers, B.A. (2020) 'Researching while queer: A research note about a genderqueer lesbian conducting qualitative research in the southeastern United States', *International Journal of Social Research Methodology* 24(1): 31–37.

Rogers-Shaw, C., Choi, J. and Carr-Chellman, D.J. (2021) 'Understanding and managing the emotional labor of qualitative research', *Forum Qualitative Sozialforschung/Forum: Qualitative Social Research* 22(3): Art. 22. http://dx.doi.org/10.17169/fqs-22.3.3652.

de Roock, R.S. (2019) 'Digital selves, material bodies, and participant research tools: Towards material semiotic video ethnography', *International Journal of Social Research Methodology* 23(2): 119–213.

Rosenthal, G. (2018) *Interpretive Social Research: An Introduction*, Göttingen: University of Göttingen.

Ross, L.E. (2017) 'An account from the inside: Examining the emotional impct of qualitative research through the lens of "insider" research', *Qualitative Psychology* 4(3): 326–337.

Roulston, K. (2019a) 'Introduction: Examining the social practices of interviewing', in K. Roulston (ed) *Interactional Studies of Qualitative Research Interviews*, 3–27, John Benjamins.

Roulston, K. (ed) (2019b) *Interactional Studies of Qualitative Research Interviews*, Amsterdam: John Benjamins.

Ruan, N. (2020) 'Interviewing elite women professors: Methodological reflections with feminist research ethics', *Qualitative Research* 22(1): 110–125.

Rutakumwa, R., Mugisha, J.O., Bernays, S., Kabunga, E., Tumwekwase, G., Mbonye, M. and Seeley, J. (2020) 'Conducting in-depth interviews with and without voice recorders: A comparative analysis', *Qualitative Research* 20(5): 565–581.

Safron, C. (2020) '"Magazines make me uncomfortable": Discomforting, disruptive, and productive affects with youth in an urban after-school program', *Qualitative Research in Sport, Exercise and Health*. https://doi.org/10.1080/2159676X.2020.1858148.

Salmons, J. (2015) *Qualitative Online Interviews: Strategies, Design, and Skills*, 2nd edn, Thousand Oaks, CA: Sage Publications.

Sampson, H. and Johannessen, I.A. (2019) 'Turning on the tap: The benefits of using "real-life" vignettes in qualitative research interviews', *Qualitative Research* 20(1): 56–72.

Savage, M. (2010) *Identities and Social Change in Britain since 1940: The Politics of Method*, Oxford: Oxford University Press.

Scheurich, J.J. (2013) *Research Method in the Postmodern*, London and New York: Routledge.

Sim, J., Saunders, B., Waterfield, J. and Kingstone, T. (2018) 'Can sample size in qualitative research be determined a priori?', *International Journal of Social Research Methodology* 21(5): 619–634.

Smith, L.T. (2021) *Decolonising Methodologies: Research and Indigenous Peoples*, 3rd edn, London and New York: Zed Books.

Spradley, J.P. (1979) *The Ethnographic Interview*, Fort Worth, TX: Harcourt Brace.

Stewart, D.W. and Shamdasani, P. (2017) 'Online focus groups', *Journal of Advertising* 46(1): 48–60.

Tarrant, A., Way, L. and Ladlow, L. (2021) '"Oh sorry I've muted you!": Issues of connection and connectivity in qualitative (longitudinal) research with young fathers and family support professionals', *International Journal of Social Research Methodology*. https://doi.org /10.1080/13645579.2021.1986313.

Tauri, J.M. (2017) 'Research ethics, informed consent and the disempowerment of First Nation peoples', *Research Ethics* 14(3): 1–14.

Thambinathan, V. and Kinsella, E.A. (2021) 'Decolonizing methodologies in qualitative research: Creating spaces for transformative praxis', *International Journal of Qualitative Methods* 20: 1–9.

Thompson, P. and Bornat, J. (2017) *The Voice of the Past: Oral History*, 4th edn, Oxford: Oxford University Press.

Thunberg, S. and Arnell, L. (2021) 'Pioneering the use of technologies in qualitative research: A research review of the use of digital interviews', *International Journal of Social Research Methodology*. https://doi.org /10.1080/13645579.2021.1935565.

Thwaites, R. (2017) '(Re)Examining the feminist interview: Rapport, gender "matching", and emotional labour', *Frontiers in Sociology*: https://doi.org/10.3389/fsoc.2017.00018.

Tong, R. and Botts, T.F. (2018) *Feminist Thought: A More Comprehensive Introduction*, 5th edn, Boulder, CO: Westview Press.

Tierney, W.G. and Lanford, M. (2019) 'Life history methods', in *SAGE Research Methods Foundations*, London: Sage.

Treanor, M.C., Patrick, R. and Wenham, A. (2021) 'State of the art: Qualitative longitudinal research: From monochrome to technicolour', *Social Policy and Society* 20(4): 635–651.

Vandenburghe, F. (2014) *What's Critical About Critical Realism? Essays in Reconstructive Social Theory*, London and New York: Routledge.

Vila-Henninger, L., Dupuy, C., Van Ingelgom, V., Caprioli, M., Teuber, F., Pennetreau, D., Bussi, M. and Le Gall, C. (2022) 'Abductive coding: Theory building and qualitative (re)analysis', *Sociological Methods and Research*. https://journals.sagepub.com/doi/pdf/10.1177 /00491241211067508.

Vist, T. (2018) 'Toddler encounters as aesthetic interviews? Discussing an arts-based data gathering', *Qualitative Inquiry* 25(7): 604–614.

Walker, C. and Baxter, J. (2019) 'Method sequence and dominance in mixed methods research: A case study of the social acceptance of wind energy literature', *International Journal of Qualitative Methods* 18: 1–14.

Wallman, S. (1984) *Eight London Households*, London and New York: Tavistock Publications.

Weitzel, A. and Reiter, H. (2012) *The Problem-centred Interview: Principles and Practice*, London: Sage.

Weller, S. (2017) 'Using internet video calls in qualitative (longitudinal) interviews: Some implications for rapport', *International Journal of Social Research Methodology* 20(6): 613–625.

Wengraf, T. (2008) 'Biographic-narrative interpretive method (BNIM) for researching lived experience and whole lives: A summary', https://www.jiscmail.ac.uk/cgi-bin/webadmin?A3=ind0812&L =BIOGRAPHIC-NARRATIVE-BNIM&E=base64&P=890501&B=--- ---%3D_NextPart_000_003F_01C961CD.F2E03660&T=application %2Fmsword;%20name=%22B%20-%20Summary%20of%20BNIM .4.doc%22&N=B%20-%20Summary%20of%20BNIM.4.doc &attachment=q&XSS=3.

Whitaker, E.M. and Atkinson, P. (2020) 'Response to Hughes, Hughes, Sykes and Wright', *International Journal of Social Research Methodology* 23(6): 757–758. https://doi.org/10.1080/13645579.2020 .1806591.

Whyte, W.F. (1993 [1943]) *Street Corner Society: The Social Structure of an Italian Slum*, 4th edn, Chicago, IL: University of Chicago Press.

Wiles, R. (2012) *What Are Qualitative Research Ethics?* London: Bloomsbury.

Williams, M. (2016) 'Positivism', in M. Williams (ed) *Key Concepts in the Philosophy of Social Research*, 160–4, Los Angeles, CA and London: Sage.

Wilson, K., Coen, S.E., Piaskoski, A. and Gilliland, J.A. (2019) 'Children's perspectives on neighbourhood barriers and enablers to active school travel: A participatory mapping study', *The Canadian Geographer* 63(1): 112–128.

Yanow, D. and Schwartz-Shea, P. (2014) *Interpretation and Method: Empirical Research Methods and the Interpretive Turn*, 2nd edn, New York: M.E. Sharp.

Young, C., Zubrzycki, J. and Plath, D. (2021) 'The slow interview? Developing key principles and practices', *Qualitative Research* 21(4): 481–497.

INDEX